Hit and Run
BASEBALL

Rod Delmonico, MEd
Head Baseball Coach, University of Tennessee

D1125662

Leisure Press
Champaign, Illinois

Library of Congress Cataloging-in-Publication Data

Delmonico, Rod, 1958-
    Hit and run baseball / Rod Delmonico.
        p.   cm.
    Includes index.
    ISBN 0-88011-327-8
    1. Baseball--Coaching.   2. Base running (Baseball)   3. Batting
(Baseball)   I. Title.
    GV875.5.D45   1992
    796.357'07'7--dc20   9143935
                                                                              CIP

ISBN: 0-88011-327-8

Acquisitions Editor: Brian Holding
Developmental Editors: Lori Garrett, June Decker
Assistant Editors: Laura Bofinger, Elizabeth Bridgett, Dawn Levy
Copyeditor: Barbara Walsh
Proofreader: Kari Nelson
Indexer: Sheila Ary
Production Director: Ernie Noa
Typesetter: Angela K. Snyder
Text Design: Keith Blomberg
Text Layout: Denise Lowry
Cover Design: Jack Davis
Cover Photo: Nick Myers
Interior Photos: Nick Myers, Pepper Martin, Chip Baker
Printer: United Graphics

Leisure Press books are available at special discounts for bulk purchase
for sales promotions, premiums, fund-raising, or educational use. Special
editions or book excerpts can also be created to specification. For details,
contact the Special Sales Manager at Leisure Press.

Printed in the United States of America

10   9   8   7   6   5   4   3   2   1

Leisure Press
A Division of Human Kinetics Publishers, Inc.
Box 5076, Champaign, IL 61825-5076
1-800-747-4457

Canada Office:
Human Kinetics Publishers, Inc.
P.O. Box 2503, Windsor, ON N8Y 4S2
1-800-465-7301 (in Canada only)

Europe Office:
Human Kinetics Publishers (Europe) Ltd.
P.O. Box IW14
Leeds LS16 6TR
England
0532-781708

Children are a gift from God;
they are his reward. Ps. 127:3

This book is affectionately dedicated to my sons, Tony and Joey—my two greatest accomplishments.

Contents

Chapter 8: Sliding   **143**

Foreword

Good baseball teams don't wait for something to happen—they make it happen. And *Hit and Run Baseball* shows you how.

I'm quite familiar with Rod Delmonico and his style of aggressive baseball. For 6 years he was an assistant coach at Florida State under Mike Martin. The Seminoles and my Miami Hurricanes have an intense rivalry. Both teams play aggressively, pressuring the opponent's defense as much as possible. In fact, Florida State–Miami games could have served as clinics for the information in *Hit and Run Baseball*.

Rod, now the head coach at the University of Tennessee, tells you how to take advantage of your half of the inning. He shows you that you don't need big home-run hitters to score lots of runs. Instead, you can make things happen by moving the ball around the field with controlled hitting and bunting and then aggressively running the bases.

You'll learn the basics of all of the offensive skills—hitting, bunting, baserunning, reading pitchers, stealing, and sliding. The skills are emphasized with 25 drills.

In his hitting chapter, Rod covers the basics of bat selection, grip, stance, location in the batter's box, stride, and swing. He gives additional information on hitting to the opposite field, correcting errors in a hitter's swing, and mentally preparing to hit.

There's more to bunting than the sacrifice bunt, and Rod shows you how to drag, push, fake, and squeeze bunt.

On the bases, you'll learn not only how to take a lead, return to base, steal bases, and advance from one base to the next, but also how to read pitchers—vital for any runner who wants to put pressure on a defense.

Finally, Rod shows how to safely execute slides—bent-leg, pop-up, hook, flip-flop, and head-first.

Most teams can't afford to wait for the big inning. Often, it never comes. I encourage you to master the skills and strategies of *Hit and Run Baseball*. When you do, you'll be on your way not only to playing aggressive base-ball—but to winning baseball.

Ron Fraser
Head Baseball Coach
University of Miami

Preface

*I*n baseball there are basically two types of coaches: one that waits for things to happen, and the other that *makes* things happen. The coach can control the game with a bunt, a steal, or an aggressive baserunning tactic. Whether the team is ahead, tied, or behind, the coach should always be maneuvering with an offensive tactic to keep the defense on edge. Using creativity in the coaching box and going against the traditional coaching strategy can literally win ball games.

It is for this reason that I wrote *Aggressive Baseball* for coaches at all levels. The information in this book is designed to aid the coach and player in developing an aggressive offense. Both the coach and player will be able to develop the necessary skills from this book to enhance their own offensive game. Over 200 photos and diagrams help illustrate the proper techniques of each specific task. I also provide specific drills in each chapter to help you put theory into practice. Each chapter also has a section on the often-overlooked mental aspects of the game.

Good hitting is essential if your players are to score, and chapter 1 is devoted to this. Hitters who use the entire field to hit make things very difficult for an opposing pitcher. Making contact and driving the baseball hard somewhere will be very effective. That pesky little hitter who keeps fouling balls off until the pitcher walks him or gives up a base hit will drive teams crazy. Don't wait for the big inning. In many of our games we have had one or two hits and three or four runs. The mark of a good aggressive offense is the same number of runs as hits.

Every baseball player can learn to do two things well: Bunt and run bases. My offensive approach to the game is built on these two essential skills. My philosophy is to make things happen by being aggressive on the base paths. The aggressive coach believes in this philosophy and instills it in his players. It starts at the top and has a trickle-down effect through the players. An aggressive team will put pressure on the defense and create uncertainty.

If a player bunts well, you'll find the opposing infielders moving in a couple of steps, and that will usually cause them to lose a step or two laterally. Chapter 2 is dedicated to improving your team's bunting.

If your players bunt well and run aggressively, you will find the infielders charging ground balls and rushing their throws. Result: a lot of bobbles and bad throws. The aggressive running game will also cause the outfielders to bobble ground balls and hurry their throws to the infield, giving the runner(s) a chance to take an extra base. With the information provided in chapter 3, players will easily get to first and maybe beyond. The material presented in chapters 4, 5, 6, and 8 (including how to read the pitcher for giveaways) ensures that base runners will go from first to third without hesitation, adding to the defense's frustration. Chapter 7 tells you how to get those runners home.

Your team's aggressive running can affect almost every aspect of your opponent's game. With aggressive runners on base, the inexperienced pitcher is going to lose his concentration and deliver fat pitches to the hitters. Coaches also tend to tighten up against an aggressive running team and to start overmanaging, calling too many pickoff plays. Result: frustration, tension, and errors.

Remember, baseball games are won or lost in the seventh, eighth, and ninth innings, and the team that makes the least errors or puts the most pressure on the defense, either physically or mentally, usually wins the game. The aggressive approach causes the defense to make mistakes.

For example: eighth inning in a tie game, an aggressive team hits a ground ball to the second baseman and he bobbles it . . . and you can just feel the aggressive offense turn it on. It is going to make something happen, and then look out! It will take advantage of the infielder kicking a ground ball. A steal, sacrifice, fly ball, and now the team has the lead, or better yet, the winning run.

Significantly, during the time I coached there, Florida State used to be a club that played for the big inning. It seemed to work—during the regular season. In postseason play, however, when good pitching dominates good hitting, we had to struggle to score runs. In 1985, for example, we hit 143 home runs but had trouble scoring in a regional tournament and were quickly eliminated.

It was evident that we had to change our offensive philosophy, and so we switched to an aggressive running game. The results were dramatic. Over the past few years, Florida State has either led the nation in stolen bases or been in the top five. We finished second in the 1986 College World Series, fifth in 1987, and third in 1989.

As head coach at the University of Tennessee, I have also been very successful in making something happen by being aggressive on the base paths. Each year we are at the top of the Southeastern Conference in team stolen bases. We led the conference in 1990 and 1991.

As the coach, you have more control of the game than you may realize. The purpose of *Aggressive Baseball* is to show you how to improve your game by adopting an aggressive style. Armed with knowledge gleaned from this book and a fresh, take-charge attitude toward the game, you can help your team consistently succeed.

My credo now is, "Don't wait for something to happen; go out and make it happen. Winners *make* it happen . . . losers *let* it happen."

Acknowledgments

First and foremost, I would like to extend my deep appreciation to Herman Mason, whose extensive assistance, talented editing, and counsel helped mold this project into its final form.

I also owe great thanks to Coach Bill Wilhelm, for believing in me as a 21-year-old coach under his helm; Turtle Thomas, who ignited the fire in me to begin writing; and Mike Martin, for his 6 years of invaluable leadership at Florida State University.

Many thanks also to the photographers—Earl "Pepper" Martin, Chip Baker, and Nick Myers—and to the many players who posed for the photographs.

And last, but certainly not least, for her long, hard hours of typing, editing, and proofreading, I owe great thanks to my wife, Barbara. Without her, this book would not have been possible.

CHAPTER 1

Hitting

Probably the most difficult skill of all sports is hitting a baseball. Think about it for a moment. You have to swing a round bat at a small round ball coming in at 85 to 90 miles per hour, and you have to time it so that you establish contact just out in front of the plate.

It might not be so bad if the ball came straight in, but more often than not it will suddenly break in, or break out, sink, or maybe even rise.

The ability to establish consistent contact takes a lot of doing—constant study and an enormous amount of practice. Is there a best way of hitting a baseball? Answer: Some of the experts *think* there is, but there is no one foolproof system of hitting.

Coaches interested in evolving a scientific approach to hitting are confronted with a mass of contradictory information. Our hitting gurus disagree on practically everything, while our scientists believe only in arcane theories that nobody but other scientists can understand.

Whom do you believe? The expert who tells you to swing a little up on the ball or the one who tells you to swing a little down? Do you extend your arms and meet the ball out in front of the plate, as decreed by almost all of the experts? Or do you try to meet the ball just inside the front foot, with the front arm fairly straight but the back arm flexed at the elbow, as a lot of smart young coaches are beginning to teach?

About the word "extend": It is probably the most abused term in hitting. Extension means thrusting the arms straight out. Do you really want your hitters to do that? Check this out with your biomechanics professor or physics expert. You will learn that extending the arms is no way to get the most out of your swing.

If you have access to motion-picture sequences of experienced hitters, check the point of contact. You will find that the ball is usually met just inside the front foot with the back arm clearly bent at contact.

Question: With so many conflicting theories in force, how can the high school or college coach go about teaching players to hit? I believe that the amateur coach should avoid adopting any scientific system of hitting, like the Lau method or the Williams method. I don't think that our kids are ready for it or that the coach has the time to work on it with each hitter.

The best way to teach hitting is by focusing on basic concepts (a point on which everyone agrees). Once the hitter has developed a good, solid foundation, he can build from there. He can go on to experiment with different ideas, perhaps a little better suited to his growing body, strength, and experience.

Let us see how these sound, basic fundamentals, called the "absolutes" of hitting, can be taught to your hitters and how they can make good, consistent hitters out of everyone.

IN GENERAL

All good hitters have at least two things in common: They are aggressive and they can concentrate. You can talk technique all you want, but if your hitters cannot concentrate and are not aggressive, they will never become good hitters. Once the hitter steps into the batter's box, he must be physically and mentally ready to hit, all geared up to meet the ball with authority and consistency.

Every hitter will be a little different in his approach. Some of the better hitters may even have flaws. Some may not hold their hands right, or stride correctly, or even shift their weight according to sacred tenet. Call them "freaks," if you will, but a certain inherent ability will enable them to overcome their weaknesses.

The coach shouldn't be too ready to change them or give up on them. If the hitter is producing, the smart coach will let him do it his own way.

At the same time, the coach must evaluate every hitter to make sure nothing is impeding his progress—that the hitter is living up to his potential. If the hitter needs extra work on his basics, fine. The coach should give it to him, but he must be sure not to overcoach him.

COACHING POINT

The coach should adjust to the hitter rather than have the hitter adjust to him.

I am totally opposed to cloning hitters, making them all look alike. I believe that the cloning process takes away from the hitter's natural ability. It's extremely important for the hitter to listen to your ideas and philosophy and *then* personalize them—adapt them to his own ability.

BAT SELECTION

The first specific consideration is the choice of bat. The hitter should look for a bat that feels comfortable and that he can drive through the strike zone. The chief danger to avoid is the heavy bat. Little Leaguers are especially guilty of this. They believe that the heavier the bat, the farther they will be able to drive the ball. They don't understand that it isn't the weight of the bat that counts, but rather the speed with which the bat is swung. The batter must be able to drive it easily and quickly through the strike zone.

That is why most hitters are using much lighter bats than hitters did in the old days. The average major-league hitter uses a bat about 33 to 34 inches long and weighing 32 to 35 ounces.

GRIP

After selecting his bat, the hitter must think of grip. He must make sure to grip the bat in the fingers. Check Figure 1.1 to see how the bat is gripped in the fingers, not in the palms or jammed toward the back part of the hands.

Figure 1.1

To get this point over to the hitter, have him put the left index finger into the palm of the right hand and grip it tightly. Then have him try to pull it out. It will come out quite easily. Now have him put the left index finger into the fingers of the right hand and tighten the grip. Then have him try to pull the index finger out. It will be a lot harder to do.

There are two theories on how the hitter should position his hands. First, he can line up the middle knuckles of both hands. Look again at Figure 1.1 and see how I've outlined the knuckles by drawing a line on the batting gloves. I happen to prefer this way of aligning the knuckles.

The other and perhaps more popular method is to line up the middle knuckles of the top hand between the first and second knuckles of the bottom hand. See Figure 1.2.

Figure 1.2

Holding the bat in the fingers with the knuckles aligned as shown will give the hitter all the flexibility he needs in his wrists. The opposite is true when the bat is held back in the palms. That will cause the hitter to lock his wrists and prevent him from swinging the bat freely.

STANCE

Though stances vary from player to player, all have certain basics.

Width

Generally, the feet should never be more than shoulder-width apart. That width provides the most comfort and the best "launching pad" for the swing.

An overly wide stance tends to inhibit the weight transfer, whereas an overly narrow stance tends to produce an overly long stride and a poor weight shift.

Horizontal Placement of Feet

The hitter can set his front foot in one of three positions: (1) closer to the plate than the back foot—*closed* stance; (2) farther away from the plate than the back foot—*open* stance; (3) exactly on line with the back foot—*square* stance.

Certainly a lot of outstanding hitters hit from either a closed or an open stance. See Figure 1.3. But if you want hitters to learn the proper mechanics, you'd do well to have them stay away from these two extremes.

Figure 1.3a   **b**

The square stance will put a player in the best position to hit. Check Figure 1.4. Note that the hands are not too high and not too low, and that the elbows are pointing

Figure 1.4

down. You don't want the back elbow to point up. That will create tension in the elbow and hurt the hitter's swing.

I don't like the open stance because it makes it difficult to cover the outside of the plate. And I don't like the closed stance because it makes it difficult to rotate the hips, making the hitter vulnerable to inside pitches (jamming him).

To give the devil his due, however, the open stance does give the hitter a better view of the pitch and can help him pull the ball to his strong side, whereas the closed stance gives him a better shot at the outside pitch and can help him hit to the opposite field.

Vertical Placement of Feet

It is important for the hitter to keep the back foot parallel to the back line of the batter's box. In fact, it may be of some benefit to turn the back foot in slightly. Remember, the hitter will have to pivot on the back foot, and this will be easier to do with the back foot turned in rather than out. The slight turn (no more than 45 degrees) will ensure the proper rotation.

The front foot should be kept parallel with the front line of the batter's box with the toe pointing toward the plate or maybe turned out a bit.

READY POSITION

The knees should be slightly flexed, with the body weight distributed 60 percent/40 percent over the feet, with the 60 percent over the back foot, which allows the hitter to stay back a little longer. The batter should lean slightly forward over the balls of the feet for balance.

The upper body should be slightly bent at the waist, with the head turned toward the pitcher and the eyes focused on him. The hands (holding the bat) should be kept no more than 3 to 8 inches away from the body, just off the back shoulder. The lead shoulder should be pointed at the pitcher, or slightly closed (turned in). The elbows must be pointed down at the ground in a relaxed position.

When the body is positioned as just described, the player is in ready position. Figure 1.5a shows the hitter in a good ready position, and Figure 1.5b offers a side view of the hitter's stance.

Figure 1.5a   b

BAT POSITION

Note that the bat is held at a 45-degree angle rather than straight up and down. The angled position allows the hitter to take the bat straight to the ball with no wasted movement. The hitter who holds the bat straight up and down will usually have to loop the bat, causing a long, slower swing.

The upright bat position is for the big fellows who can hit for power. The flat position is generally for the smaller hitters who are not concerned with power.

The hitter should always take a few practice swings to stay loose and relaxed, and should keep his hands and body loose rather than stiff and tense to assure a "quick" bat.

LOCATION IN BOX

Every good hitter has his own ideas on where to stand in the batter's box. Several important basics come into play here. The closer you stand to the plate, the quicker you'll usually have to be on an inside pitch. The deeper you stand in the box, the more trouble you'll have on breaking balls.

The closer you stand to the front of the box, the quicker you will again have to be. If you choose to stand away from the plate, the more you will have to guard the outside part of the plate. Remember, you will be giving the pitcher an area—the outside part of the plate—to work on. A pitcher with a sharp breaking pitch can be very cruel to hitters who give him a lot of the outside part of the plate.

If you have extremely quick hands, you may want to stay closer to the plate. If your hands happen to be slower, you may find it easier to set up a little farther from the plate.

COACHING POINT

It's important for a hitter to find the position in the batter's box that goes along with his particular makeup.

Rod Carew made adjustments in the batter's box according to the pitcher. Not every hitter can do this, of course. I would suggest that every hitter find a position that will help him obtain complete plate coverage.

Notice in Figure 1.6 that the hitter is in the middle of the box—not too far and not too close, not too much in front

Figure 1.6

or too much in back of the box. Also note that his front foot comes to rest a few inches in front of the plate after his stride.

STRIDE

We have all seen hitters with a picture-perfect stance, good hand-eye coordination, and great athletic ability fail to live up to their potential because of their poor weight transfer. I believe that weight shift is the most important aspect of hitting, outside of focus on the ball.

As the pitcher starts his windup, the hitter should start his trigger, or cocking, action. He must begin rotating his front shoulder, hip, and knee inward. This slight inward rotation of the entire front side will cause the hands to cock no more than 3 to 4 inches backward.

Notice Figure 1.7. As the front side turns inward, the weight must shift back to the back leg, and the hitter must take a short step with his front foot—no more than 6 to 8 inches. Many hitters will stride on the big toe or inside part of the front foot to help keep the weight back.

Figure 1.8 shows the front heel slightly off the ground, allowing the hitter to keep his weight back until the swing is initiated.

Remember, a hitter should stride *to* hit, not stride *and* hit at the same time. Many hitters will jump or lunge at

Figure 1.7a   **b**

Figure 1.8

the ball, shifting their weight too quickly to the front foot, as shown in Figure 1.9. I call this fault lunging. In short, as the hitter strides, his hands go forward and his front side doesn't rotate inward to a cocked position. He thus gives up hand speed or, in essence, a quick bat. Notice how much the head moves forward, and where the hands end up—in a very weak position. Two bad things can happen to this kind of hitter: He can be fooled by off-speed pitches or jammed by inside fastballs.

Figure 1.10 presents a front view of the hitter stepping and cocking his hands to the trigger position. This action,

Figure 1.9a   b

Figure 1.10a   b

properly timed, keeps the hitter from jumping or using an unnecessary amount of movement before the swing.

At this point, the stride should be completed, with the front foot closed rather than pointing at the pitcher. The hitter must avoid opening his front foot, because his hip will fly out and he will lose the cocked or *strong* position of the front side. The problem will start at the foot and end with the head flying open and the hitter losing sight of the ball.

At the completion of the stride, the weight should be on the inside part of the back foot (see Figure 1.11). Notice how the hands are in the trigger position just off the back shoulder at the top of the strike zone.

The hitter is now ready to go to the final phase—the swing.

Figure 1.11

SWING

The swing is not begun with the arms. It is initiated by the legs and hips. As the hitter begins to move his weight forward to the front foot, he pivots on the back foot (to permit a maximum effort from the hips) and begins to turn on the back knee. Figure 1.12 shows how the front foot remains straight.

The normal opening of the shoulders helps the hands come down and through.

COACHING POINT

The hitter must keep his shoulder from opening up too soon. The hitter who opens up too soon will have trouble handling the outside pitch, and he will also find it difficult to hit the off-speed pitch with any degree of consistency.

It is extremely important for the hitter to keep the head still and focused on the baseball during the swing.

Figure 1.12a   **b**   **c**

As the hitter starts bringing his arms and hands forward, he keeps the lead elbow pointed down toward the ground (see Figure 1.13). The elbow should not come up to or above the shoulders, because this will drop the barrel of the bat below the hands and cause an uppercut swing.

To repeat: The hitter should keep the barrel of the bat above his hands during the swing. This will ensure a short, quick swing that will take the barrel directly to the ball. As the bat moves into the hitting zone, it will normally become parallel to the ground.

Figure 1.13

In a good swing, the hands will come inside and then extend on every pitch. Notice in Figure 1.14 how the hands are in close to the body. They will simply extend at the time of contact.

Figure 1.14

Whenever the arms are extended too early in the swing, the swing will be too long and cause a loss of power. On an outside pitch, the hands will leave the body sooner than they would on an inside pitch. As the hands move closer to the contact area, the palm of the top hand will face up and the palm of the bottom hand will face down.

The hips and shoulders continue to drive against a now firm front leg, as the back toe begins to turn toward the pitcher. The lead arm remains straight and the back arm stays bent (at the elbow) at contact. The head is slightly bowed toward the plate as the bat meets the ball.

As the hitter drives through the baseball, he should imagine himself hitting three baseballs back to back. Some hitters will often hit the ball and then cut off their swing, causing them to hit under the ball and pop it up.

But if the hitter will go through the ball and feel as if he has hit three baseballs back to back, he'll tend to hit line drives more often than not.

Teaching little guys—10-, 11-, and 12-year-olds—to hit the ball down and through will ingrain the basic mechanics so that when they get bigger and stronger they will be able to slightly adjust their swing and lift the ball—drive it—in the air more often.

Even a player with the ability to hit the ball out of the ballpark should be forced to concentrate on hitting line-drive and ground balls. Remember, the easiest ball to catch is a fly ball. Kids who learn to hit line drives and grounders will not only win ball games but also will learn to hit for average. They will continue to force the defense to catch the ball, throw it, catch it again, and tag a base to get them out. By putting pressure on the defense, they will be making something happen . . . perhaps forcing an error.

The hitter derives his power from the hips and his quickness from the hands. When the lower half and upper half of the body begin working together, the hitter will develop a good, short, quick swing and gain extra power from the hips.

After the hitter has hit the baseball and completed the swing, I believe it's natural for him to let go of the top hand and continue to follow through with the bat. The release of the top hand will give the hitter an opportunity to finish his swing and keep from pulling his head out.

In summary: Let every player personalize the basic areas. One hitter may want to hold his hands a little higher; another hitter may want to stride a little more; one hitter may choose a wider stance; another may bend over a little more. Each hitter is going to be different. Don't fight them! Don't "fix" anything unless it is broken.

Nevertheless, many of the basics of the stance, stride, and swing should remain the same for everyone. Every hitter must have a cocking action, keep his weight back, swing down and through the baseball, use his hips and pivot on his back foot, and visually track the baseball to get the most out of his mechanics and to groove a consistent swing.

HITTING FAULTS AND CORRECTIONS

Certain problems or faults will impair the swing and make for inconsistency. Following is a list of common faults and how to correct and help eliminate them.

Fault	*Correction*
Overstriding	Have the hitter spread out and hit without using a stride, or stride on the ball of the lead foot.
No pivot on back foot	The hitter should raise the heel of the back foot off the ground a little and turn the back foot in a little.
Pulling head and front shoulder out	Have a pitcher throw to a catcher while the hitter visually tracks the ball.
Swinging late	Instruct the hitter to start the cocking action sooner.
Front elbow comes up and out	Have the hitter put a batting glove under his front armpit and swing without allowing the glove to fall to the ground.
Swing is too long	Have the hitter bring the hands a little closer to the body. He should also practice the Quick-Hand Drill.
Hips don't rotate	The hitter should practice the Quick-Hand Drill, the Tire Drill, and pivoting on the back foot while working on a tee. (See end of chapter for these drills.)
Hands extend too early	The Wall Drill is excellent to develop an inside-out swing.
Dropping hands or hitching	Have the hitter put his bat on his shoulder and then lift his hands up and back to the trigger position.
Stops swing	The Tire Drill is excellent to develop a good follow-through.

COACHING POINT

As a coach, you may want to think twice about telling your hitters to "take" the first pitch or "look for the walk." This can have a negative effect on young hitters, discouraging them from being aggressive. Always remember who you are and where you're coaching: You are coaching kids—so don't expect them to perform like big leaguers!

Mental Aspects for Players

The mental part of hitting is probably the most difficult phase to coach. The ideal type of hitter will take an 0 for 4 with the same kind of equanimity that he takes a 4 for 4.

What you are looking for, and always working on, are maturity, poise, confidence, toughness, and aggressiveness. Very few young athletes will be able to develop *all* of these qualities, but they can develop enough of them to make them strong, consistent hitters.

I want my players to be constantly alert, constantly studying the game, and constantly working with and supporting their teammates.

I believe in using videotapes to evaluate players and get to know them individually so that when a player gets into a certain groove, I will know how it has happened and will be able to stay on top of the situation.

Here are several ideas that every hitter should mentally practice over the course of a season.

- Know the type of pitcher you are facing.
- Always look for the fastball and then adjust to a curveball.
- Look for the pitch away and then adjust to the pitch inside.
- Know the strike zone, but be ready to adjust to the *umpire's* strike zone.
- Be aware of the game situation each time at bat.

- Study the pitcher while you're in the dugout and the on-deck circle.
- Take the first pitch if the two previous hitters have been retired on three or fewer total pitches.
- When you take a pitch, track the ball all the way to the catcher's glove.
- Because you hit only four or, at the most, five times a game, make each turn at bat something special to you.
- Before the game starts, watch the pitcher in the bull pen to see what he has working and not working for him.
- With every pitch you are thinking, yes, yes, yes, no (ball) on the swing.
- With two strikes, choke up a little on the bat for control.
- Don't take the same swing with two strikes that you do with no strikes; shorten up a little.
- Try to hit the change-up to the opposite field.
- Step out of the box any time the pitcher is working too fast for you.
- If you can't pick up the signal from the third-base coach, call time and walk out to meet him.
- On 3-0, you may think of "zoning" the pitcher—swinging at any pitch that goes into the area of the strike zone you have mapped out in your mind. Anything else, let go through.

HITTING DRILLS

There are no deep, dark secrets about good hitting. Nor are there any shortcuts to the magic .300 batting circle. Good hitters get there in different ways. But all of them have one thing in common: a tremendous work ethic. Every good hitter works at his craft—hard, long, and all the time.

In short, anyone who wants to become a great hitter must dedicate himself to practice and develop good practice habits. He doesn't have to take actual batting practice all the time. He can also get into a batting cage (by himself or with a partner) and focus on all the mechanics that go into a smooth, mechanically sound, grooved swing.

At the University of Tennessee, players spend at least an hour a day in the cage. Hitting is taught with drills such as the T, Flip, Soft Toss, and others. Each drill focuses on a specific area such as hands, head, hips, legs, stride, weight shift, cocking of the bat, and driving the ball to the opposite field.

It is easier to focus on these areas in a cage rather than in actual batting practice. The cage drills can prepare the hitter for practice against live pitching or can complement the actual hitting.

The hitter who doesn't have an organized practice every day can work on these drills on his own, in a batting cage or even in a backyard. (Example: The hitter can hang up a net and hit tennis balls into it off a tee.)

The hitter who is willing to spend hours working on a short, quick stroke will reap the benefits when he goes up against live pitching.

I believe that every hitter on every level of the game can profit enormously from the drills in use at Tennessee to develop good batting strokes and consistent hitters.

DRILLS

T Drill

PURPOSE: To teach the hitter to contact the ball with a smooth, compact ("grooved") swing.

EQUIPMENT: Net, batting tee, bat, balls, home plate

IMPLEMENTATION:

1. Purchase a batting tee, or make one out of radiator hose, pipes, and a wooden base.
2. Place a home plate base directly behind the tee so that the player can orient his stance to a plate rather than a tee.
3. Have the players pair up so that one (the "feeder") places the ball on the tee while the other hits (see Figure 1.15).
4. Keep moving the tee to different areas in front of the plate to give the hitter practice hitting the inside pitch, the outside pitch, and the pitch down the middle.
5. Raise the tee to different heights to give the hitter practice hitting high pitches and low pitches.

Figure 1.15

Flip Drill

PURPOSE: To teach weight transfer, body control, and timing.

EQUIPMENT: Batting cage, 5-by-5-foot net, bat, balls

IMPLEMENTATION:

1. Set up in an area with a screened net or a batting tunnel.
2. Set up the hitter in the net or tunnel with a partner (the "feeder") kneeling about 10 feet away, just off the hitter's front knee (see Figure 1.16).
3. Have the feeder trigger the hitter's cocking action by dropping his hand just before flipping the ball. Note: This is a timing device that helps the hitter cock his hands before starting his swing.
4. If the feeder flips the ball inside, the hitter must turn on the ball and drive it to the left of the net, which simulates a hit to left field.
5. If the feeder flips the ball over the middle of the plate, the hitter must drive it right back up the middle.
6. If the feeder flips the ball to the outside part of the plate, the hitter must drive the ball to the right side of the net, which simulates a hit to right field.
7. Important: Have the feeder float the ball, not throw it on a line, to the hitter.

Figure 1.16a   **b**

Hip Drill

PURPOSE: To teach hip rotation and remaining balanced at the point of contact. This drill develops good balance in the stance, pivoting on the back foot, good balance on the swing, and driving the ball to left field (or right field for a left-hand hitter).

EQUIPMENT: Batting cage, 5-by-5-foot net, bat, balls

IMPLEMENTATION:

1. Set up the hitter at the plate with a feeder kneeling in front of him, just off his front hip (see Figure 1.17).
2. Have the feeder flip the ball toward the hitter's front hip so that the hitter can pivot and drive the ball into the net to the left.
3. Safety precaution: Warn the hitter never to hit the ball back at the feeder.
4. Have the hitter concentrate on a short, quick swing while he pivots on his back foot.
5. Have the feeder alternate high and low tosses to help the hitter learn how to adjust his hands to different pitches.

Figure 1.17a

b

Tire Drill I

PURPOSE: To help the hitter develop strong wrists, hands, and forearms by driving the bat through the tire. This drill helps the player develop the feel of driving through the baseball and develops the arms from the elbow down.

EQUIPMENT: Steel pole, tire, pin, bat for tire station

IMPLEMENTATION:

1. Take a normal tire, cut a hole through the center, set the tire on a steel fence pole, and place a pin at the bottom of the pole to allow the tire to spin (see Figure 1.18).
2. Set up the hitter alongside the tire.
3. Have the hitter cock his hands, pivot on the back foot, and drive the bat into the tire, forcing it to spin.
4. Have the batter simulate swings on an inside pitch, a pitch down the middle, and a pitch on the outside.

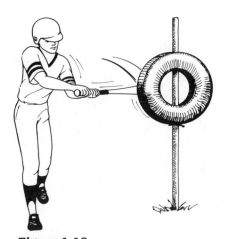

Figure 1.18

Tire Drill II

PURPOSE: To teach the player to hit the high pitch, the low pitch, or the pitch down the middle.

EQUIPMENT: Steel poles, tires, bat (see Figure 1.19)

IMPLEMENTATION:

1. Set up two steel fence poles about a foot and a half apart, and stack five tires over them as shown.
2. Have the hitter assume his stance and focus on hitting the low pitch, meaning the middle tire.
3. Next have the hitter hit tires 4 and 5, meaning the pitch down the middle and the high pitch.
4. Have the hitter concentrate on pivoting and rotating his hips as he swings and remaining balanced at contact.

Game Variation

PURPOSE: This drill teaches hand-eye coordination and helps the batter learn to adjust his swing.

IMPLEMENTATION:

1. Have the player assume his stance.
2. Have him cock the bat.
3. Have the partner call "3," "4," or "5," to let the hitter know which tire he wants him to hit.

Figure 1.19

Wall Drill

PURPOSE: To help players develop a short, quick swing that takes the bat directly to the ball. This is a great drill for a player to do while on deck waiting to hit.

EQUIPMENT: Bat, wall, fence (preferably a netted one, so that when the hitter swings he will not do any damage to his bat)

IMPLEMENTATION:

1. Have the player place the knob of the bat into his stomach and extend the bat so that the top of it touches the net (see Figure 1.20a).
2. Then have the hitter set up in his stance and take an "inside-outside" swing, with the end of the bat just barely hitting the net (see Figure 1.20b).
3. If the player swings with his arms, he will create a long, looping swing and will hit the net, keeping him from finishing his swing.

Figure 1.20a   **b**

No-Stride Drill

PURPOSE: To focus on the use of the hands in hitting, using the flip station or short toss station.

This drill teaches the hitter

- how to cock his hands,
- the importance of "staying back" (keeping the weight back),
- how to isolate the upper part of the body—the "trigger" area for the hands, and
- how to pivot and stay balanced.

EQUIPMENT: Bat, 5-by-5-foot area

IMPLEMENTATION:

1. Set up the player with his feet spread more than shoulder-width apart—about 1 to 2 feet wider than normal (see Figure 1.21a).
2. Have the player cock his bat and swing, pivoting on his back foot, as seen in Figure 1.21b. (Note: With his feet widely spread, he has no need for a stride.)
3. After the swing, have the player check to see whether he has remained on balance.

Figure 1.21a   **b**

Quick-Hand Drill

PURPOSE: To help players develop a cocking action, a pivoting action with the back foot, and a short swing. This drill helps develop quick hands and a strong leg action.

EQUIPMENT: Fence, balls

IMPLEMENTATION:

1. Set up the player in his stance with a ball in each hand (see Figure 1.22a).
2. Have the player cock both hands and then throw with a short, quick swinging action, releasing the balls at the end of the "swing" (see Figures 1.22b and c).
3. Important: Have the hitter pivot on his back foot and remain on balance.

Figure 1.22a

b

c

CHAPTER 2

Bunting

No matter how limited a baseball player's skills may be, he should be able to do at least two things well: run the bases and bunt. Every coach can use a good bunter, and the below-average player should be encouraged to work at it. It offers a good way to contribute to the success of a team.

The bunting game can add to every team's offensive versatility. The use of a varied assortment of bunts can exert enormous pressure on the defense, especially in the late innings when most games are won or lost. A sacrifice or a surprise squeeze can pull a game out of the fire.

Paradoxically, with all its advantages, bunting remains something of a lost art. Because of the long-ball syndrome and all the other things that must be worked on, many coaches refuse to allocate enough practice time to it.

There is also a psychological barrier. Sacrifice bunting is a team concept, and most players dislike the idea of giving themselves up. Watch the average practice and you'll see players lay down two foul bunts, then proceed to take 10 or 12 full swings.

So the first order of the day is to sell the bunt as a team weapon. At the University of Tennessee, countless hours of practice are spent on the technique. Every player must work on his bunting every day. Our players will actually spend an hour exclusively on bunting techniques.

Another benefit of the bunt is that many high school and even college defenses have difficulty defending it. They'll set up wrong or misplay the ball, bumbling it, or throwing it away, or throwing to the wrong base—a huge dividend for such a simple play!

That is why I teach everyone how to bunt, both for sacrificial purposes and for the base hit.

COACHING POINT

Why can't most young players bunt well? For three reasons:

1. *Poor mechanics.* **Many players aren't taught properly or fail to get enough supervised practice. Solution: Provide ample supervized practice time for bunting.**
2. *Not waiting for the proper pitch* **(strike). The player feels that once he makes up his mind to bunt, he must go through with it. Solution: Teach players that if they don't get their pitch, pull the bat back.**
3. *Rushing the play.* **The player may be in a hurry to get out of the box. Solution: The player should bunt the ball and then run.**

SACRIFICE BUNT

The sacrifice bunt is used to move a runner into scoring position. Coaches have to drill this concept into their players' heads:

"You're up there to move up the runners, period! Don't think of the base hit. Concentrate all your efforts on laying down the bunt. Let the hitters behind you drive in the run!''

COACHING POINT

The major cause of failure is trying to beat out the throw—rushing out of the box. Result: poor technique and a poor bunt.

There are basically two kinds of sacrifice bunts: the square-around and the pivot. Many coaches prefer the pivot because they feel it is a superior technique. It involves less movement, and it enables the bunter to conceal his intention longer, delaying the reaction of the defense.

At the University of Tennessee, the belief is that both styles are essential to the bunting game. For example, with a man on first base, I would use the pivot method (Figure 2.1) with a right-handed hitter and the square-around method (Figure 2.2) with a left-handed hitter.

Figure 2.1

The objective is to bunt the ball down the first-base line, about 2 feet to the inside, and force the first baseman to field the ball. As you can perceive, the left-handed hitter who squares around is going to find it much easier to bunt the ball down the line. His setup stance will give him a great angle (Figure 2.2b).

The right-handed hitter will find it easier to push the ball down the line from the pivot position (Figure 2.3). Notice how comfortable it now is for him to place the ball down the line.

Figure 2.2a   b

Figure 2.3

With runners on first and second, the objective is to get the bunt by the pitcher and force the third baseman to field it about 15 feet in front of the base. The right-hand batter will now want to sacrifice from the square-around position, whereas the left-hand hitter will want to do it via the pivot method.

Square-Around Method

After the batter has received the signal to sacrifice, he will want to move up in the box and get closer to the plate. The further up he is in the batter's box, the more fair territory he will have for the bunt. Moving closer to the plate will also give him a better chance to reach the pitch away from him.

The square-around stance puts the hitter in better position to bunt the inside pitch. He must pivot on his left foot while bringing his right foot toward the front of the box. Check Figure 2.4. Note that the hitter's shoulders are perpendicular to the pitcher and that the right foot is a little deeper than the left in a toe-to-heel relationship. Note also that the feet are slightly more than shoulder-width apart.

Figure 2.4a   b

Pivot Method

Again, the bunter wants to move up in the box and closer to the plate. As the pitcher is just about to release the ball, the right-handed bunter must take a jab step toward the first baseman with his left foot and pivot in his tracks with the right foot. Remember, a jab step is a short, quick step.

Check this movement in Figure 2.5. Notice the plate coverage that the bunter has achieved and how the front shoulder is slightly closed. Also notice that the bat in both methods is in the same position (at a 45-degree angle) at the top of the strike zone.

COACHING POINT

If a player isn't comfortable with either method, let him choose one that works best for him.

Figure 2.5a   **b**   **c**

BUNTING TECHNIQUE

After the bunter has squared or pivoted, it becomes extremely important for him to put his bat and body in the proper position.

Grip

As previously mentioned, the bat has to be placed at the top of the strike zone at a 45-degree angle. The top hand must slide up the handle toward the barrel, while the bottom hand remains put. In short, the batter should not slide both hands up the barrel, as many players do. That does not allow for much bat control. The split grip provides greater flexibility.

Now check Figure 2.6 and see the difference in the top-hand grip where the bat is cupped in the palm of the hand and the fingers are wrapped around the rear side of the bat. For younger players such as 9- to 12-year-olds, I would recommend the grip shown in Figure 2.7. It will prevent the kids from getting their fingers hit by the pitch. As the player matures, he'll obtain more bat control with the grip shown in Figure 2.6.

The bottom hand has to slide up the handle a couple of inches for a better feel. The elbows are slightly bent, in, and pointed down, and the bat is held out in front. The player pinches the bat with his thumb and index finger to prevent injury to his fingers.

Figure 2.6

Figure 2.7

COACHING POINT

You don't want the bunter to hold the bat too close to the body because this will make it difficult for him to see the bat contact the ball. The bunter must keep the bat at the top of the strike zone and out in front of his body (Figure 2.8).

Angle

The angle of the bat is a vital concern, of course. The bunter must set the angle just before the pitcher releases the ball. The bunter must decide where to bunt the ball and then immediately set the bat angle.

Figure 2.8

If bunting down the third-base line, the right-handed batter must point the barrel of the bat toward first base.

With runners on first and second, the left-handed batter must point the knob of the bat toward first base, because he wants to place the ball down the third-base line.

Perhaps one of the most important aspects of bunting is for the batter to get the bat out in front of the plate so that he may track the ball from the mound to the front of the plate. Bunters who bunt the ball out in front are going to be more consistent and have a better chance of bunting the ball fair.

Figure 2.9a   **b**

Knees

The knees must be kept slightly bent with the weight over the balls of the feet. If the pitch is thrown low, the bunter must bend his knees to get down to the ball (see Figure 2.9). It is imperative that the bunter not drop the bat head in trying to bunt the low pitch. He must bend his knees on any pitch below his hands.

Making Contact

The bunter who drops the bat head on a low pitch will usually contact the ball with the top half of the bat, causing a pop-up. The idea is to bunt the top half of the ball with the bottom half of the bat.

On a sacrifice bunt, the bunter wants the ball to drop "dead" upon hitting the ground. Coaches used to tell their bunters to "catch the ball with the bat and try to give a little." This often created contact problems and inconsistency.

There are two better ways of obtaining the deadening effect:

1. Instruct the bunter to carry the bat more in the fingers of the top hand. As the ball hits the bat, it will tend to retract the bat toward the palms of the hands, imparting a deadening effect on the ball as it comes off the bat.
2. Instruct the bunter to contact the ball more toward the end of the bat. This will really work well with a wooden bat. However, you don't want him to grip the bat too tightly with the top hand, because that will cause the ball to come off the bat too hard, and he must avoid pushing at the ball with the bat.

BUNTING FOR A HIT

A little concentrated work on drag bunting can add a lot of points to the batting average of the ordinary hitter. For example, just 10 successful bunts over the course of a season can tack 20 points onto a player's season batting average. Bunting for a base hit is an invaluable skill that will put pressure on the defense and make things happen.

The best time to bunt for a hit is when the infielders are playing deep or when the scouting report indicates that the third baseman and pitcher are poor fielders. The right-handed batter can elect to *push* the ball toward first or *drag* it down the third-base line, whereas the left-handed batter will push down toward third and drag down the first-base line. The idea is to wait until the last split second and then surprise the defense.

The batter should position himself comfortably close to the plate, because he's going to look for a pitch low and away. He should also move up in the box a few inches to give himself more fair territory to bunt in.

The essential rules for your hitters to remember when bunting for a base hit are as follows: (1) Get your pitch (middle to low and away), and (2) don't be in a hurry to run out of the box. You want them to bunt the ball and then run. Placement is more important than the jump.

Base Hit Bunts From the Right Side

The bunt down the third-base line is an especially tactical play against a third baseman playing deep. The vital strategic point for the bunter to remember is to bunt the ball close to (within 3 feet of) the line and to make the bunt "perfect or foul."

Even if the third baseman is just one step behind the base, a good bunter will often be able to beat out a bunt. Speed is a tremendous aid, but technique can compensate for just average speed. A good push or drag up the third-base line is the toughest play for a third baseman to make. And if he backs up a step on every strike, as most infielders do, so much the better. So, with one strike, the batter should not be afraid to bunt. If he bunts foul, he will still have a chance to bunt or hit again. If he bunts fair but more than 6 feet off the line, he'll probably be thrown out. Again, bunt perfect or foul!

COACHING POINT

Some bunters become afraid to bunt when they get one strike on them. Actually, this will enhance the bunting situation, because the infielders will move back a little and be more apt to look for the hitter to swing away.

Drag Bunt

Figure 2.10 shows the technique of drag bunting down the third-base line. As the pitcher delivers, the hitter must draw his bat back a little, simulating a swing. He should point the bat at the first baseman, setting the angle for a perfect bunt down third. At the same time, he should take a jab step back with the right foot.

Figure 2.10a   **b**   **c**

Note the head of the extended bat—how it points toward first base (Figure 2.11). It is important to set the angle as the bat is extended. Many young players fail to set the proper angle and wind up rotating the bat at the last second, putting a spin on the ball and causing it to go foul. Also notice the bunter's split grip. This grip provides superior bat control.

The bat has to be out in front just above the left thigh, as shown in Figure 2.11. If the bat is behind the thigh, it

Figure 2.11

will create a blind spot that makes it difficult for the hitter to establish good contact.

The head of the bat points up at the start, then points a little toward the ground at actual contact. This method allows the hitter to be more consistent.

Some players try to deaden the ball by retracting the bat. This is unnecessary. The force of the ball going down and hitting the ground will slow the ball up just enough.

COACHING POINT

If the ball is thrown in on the hands, the batter must take it. (This is also true of the push bunt.) A bunter cannot get a good start out of the box on a pitch in on the hands.

Push Bunt

The push bunt is usually used against a first baseman playing deep. The bunt is directed past the left side of the pitcher and well over to the first baseman's right. Ideally, you want the second baseman to move over and in to field the ball on the grass—a very tough play for the best of second basemen.

The push bunt is especially effective against a left-handed pitcher who keeps falling off to the right side of the mound. It becomes very hard for him to recover in time to get the ball.

The bunter should remember two rules: (1) Get the right pitch (middle to away and up), and (2) get the ball by the pitcher.

As the pitcher delivers, the batter wants to push the bat at the ball, using a firm grip with his top hand. The ball must be bunted hard enough to get by the pitcher.

As shown in Figure 2.12, the bunter should take a short jab step with his left foot and push the outside pitch toward first. The idea is to meet the ball as the right foot hits the ground.

Figure 2.12a   b

Notice that the bat is out in front above the left thigh, enabling the bunter to see the ball hit the bat. He also wants to keep the head of the bat up, which will cause the ball to go down more consistently.

After making contact with the ball, the right-handed bunter should bring his right (rear) foot over and head toward first. As previously mentioned, the bunter wants to place the ball in the hole between the pitcher and the first baseman, causing the second baseman to field the ball.

Good situations for the drag or push bunt include the following:

• When you want to help get an inning started with no one on base

- When the batter is in a slump and is looking to come out of it with some kind of hit
- With a runner on second and no outs; a push bunt will get the runner over to third with one (or maybe none) out

Base Hit Bunts From the Left Side

The left-handed hitter enjoys an advantage over the right-handed hitter. Not only is he a full step closer to first, but his swing brings him around toward the bag and thus enables him to get a quicker start.

Drag Bunt

The left-handed drag bunt is a good tactic against a first baseman who is playing deep. The idea is to bunt the ball by the pitcher and first baseman, forcing the second baseman to field the ball. If the first baseman fields the ball, it will become a foot race between pitcher and bunter.

Figure 2.13 shows a very good technique. As the pitcher delivers, the bunter rotates his hands back a little to help decoy the defense.

The first step is made with the right (front) foot toward the third baseman. Note: Most left-handed bunters will err here. They will cross over with the back foot, putting them

Figure 2.13a   **b**

in poor position to bunt the ball. The initial step with the front foot is fundamentally more sound and also makes it appear that the batter is going to swing.

As the ball approaches the plate, the bunter must slide his hands up the bat as shown and bring the bat forward.

COACHING POINT

I prefer to have the batter keep his hand down on the end of the bat and slide just the top hand up the shaft. This kind of split grip furnishes better bat control. The hands should not be held together in a closed grip. This will put the bat more at the mercy of the ball.

It is also important for the bunter to angle the bat as he brings it forward. The ball will rebound off the bat and go down the first-base line between the pitcher and the base.

The best type of pitch to drag is the strike in the middle-to-in part of the plate. This type of pitch can be seen better and also enables the bunter to keep the head of the bat up, helping the ball to stay down.

At contact, the bunter should shift his weight to his front foot and then cross his back foot over the front.

Warning: The bunter must not run out of there too quickly. Rushing creates a visual blind spot and causes inconsistency. The ball must be bunted out in front and then the back foot crossed over. It is like fielding a baseball; you have to catch the ball before you can throw it. In bunting, a player has to bunt the ball before he can run.

After the left-handed hitter has mastered this drag, he may be allowed to cross over early with his back foot directly toward the pitcher. He must still step with his left foot, then start to cross over a little sooner, allowing him to get a better jump out of the box. Remember, though, you should allow this only after he has mastered the first technique.

Push Bunt

On the left-handed push bunt, it is essential that the player bunt the ball first and then run. The bunter must stay in there longer than on the drag bunt. (He can afford to cheat a little when he drags.)

As the bunter steps into the box, he should move up a few inches to get a little more fair territory to bunt into. He should also look for a pitch up and over the plate, because the outside pitch is very difficult to bunt and get a good start on.

The first step is made with the front foot. It slides toward the third baseman as the hands go back. As the ball approaches, the bunter shifts his weight to the front foot and bunts the ball down the line.

Notice the bat angle in Figure 2.14. The bunter must place the bat at the proper angle before he meets the ball.

Figure 2.14a   b

c

The common mistake is to adjust the angle with the right hand at the last instant. This will put a peculiar spin on the ball, usually causing it to go foul.

The player who finds himself bunting the ball too hard down the line can help deaden the ball a little by moving his top hand closer to the barrel end. He can also try bunting the ball closer to the end of the bat. The force of the ball going down into the ground will also help deaden the ball. Optional method: Have the bunter hold the bat looser with the top hand, causing the bat to give a little when the ball strikes it.

The golden rule in push bunting: Bunt the ball perfectly, or else foul it off. If you bunt foul, you'll still have another chance to bunt or hit. If you make a bad bunt, the pitcher or third baseman will probably throw you out. Remember . . . perfect or foul.

A perfect bunt will go between the foul line and an imaginary line about 3 feet in fair territory. The idea is to force the third baseman to come in and make the play.

Even if the third baseman gets to the ball, he'll find it very difficult to make a play. He'll have to throw underhand, and he isn't going to get much on the throw. In fact, he'll often throw the ball away.

FAKE BUNT

When the infield is playing too close to lay down a bunt, the batter will want to show bunt or fake a bunt. This will cause the infielders to hold their "in" positioning, reducing their lateral movement and giving the hitter an opportunity to drive a ball by them.

This is also effective when a runner is stealing. The batter fakes a bunt and brings the bat back as the ball crosses the plate. The bat will block the catcher's view for a split second and may cause him to bobble or drop the ball. The fake bunt can also be used when a runner is stealing home and the hitter pivots to bunt. The rule states that the ball must be allowed to cross the plate. The catcher cannot move in front of the plate to receive the ball.

By faking the bunt, the hitter forces the catcher to receive the ball behind the plate. The runner can now slide to the front side of the plate, making it difficult for the catcher to tag him.

COACHING POINT

It is important for the batter to bring the bat back just before the ball crosses the plate.

At the University of Tennessee, I have my players fake bunt and slap on occasion, specifically with runners on first and second in a bunting situation and the defense on the move—the shortstop running to cover third while the third and first basemen are charging.

With the third baseman, the shortstop, and the second and first basemen running either left or right, they are all out of position, leaving several holes through which the hitter can slap the ball.

Another good situation for a fake bunt is with a man on third or the bases loaded. The idea now is to get the pitcher to throw a wild pitch or put himself in the hole by thinking squeeze. This is especially effective with the bases loaded and a 3-1 count on the hitter. Try to get the pitcher to lose his concentration and throw ball four.

SQUEEZE BUNTS

The main purpose of the squeeze play is for a team to score a go-ahead, a tying, or an insurance run in the late innings. It is usually a major offensive weapon for a weak-hitting club.

There are two basic types of squeeze bunts: the safety squeeze and the suicide squeeze.

Safety Squeeze

This is used with a runner on third base and one or no outs; it is a great play with one out.

As the pitcher releases the ball, the hitter must take a jab step with his lead foot—toward first base if he is a right-handed hitter and toward third base if he is a left-handed hitter.

The bunt is executed with the pivot method. The bunter's main objective is to bunt a strike. The runner breaks for home only if he can read the trajectory of the ball off the bat. It must be breaking toward the ground.

The right-handed hitter should bunt the ball down the

Figure 2.15a   **b**

first-base line, whereas the left-handed hitter should place it down the third-base line (Figure 2.15). The bunter must try to avoid bunting the ball directly back to the pitcher.

COACHING POINT

The hitter must not run out of the box. His main objective is to lay down a good bunt and enable the run to score. He must not be concerned with being thrown out.

Suicide Squeeze

The ball must be bunted no matter where it is thrown. The hitter again uses the pivot method to bunt the ball in fair territory.

The key to the success of the play is for the runner to break as the pitcher's arm comes forward, preventing the pitcher from changing the location of the pitch. If, for example, the runner tries to break as the pitcher is in his windup, the pitcher could pitch out or knock the batter down, getting the runner in a rundown for the tag out.

Cue for the bunter: Bunt the ball in fair territory and don't be concerned with placement.

COACHING POINT

As you can see, good bunting puts a lot of pressure
on the defense. But it has to be practiced over and
over. The bunter must learn how to get his bunting
technique down perfectly.

Mental Aspects for Players

Instruct your players to keep the following points in mind:

- After getting the sign for a sacrifice bunt, immediately think of where you are going to bunt the ball and the technique you are going to use.
- When sacrificing, offer only at a strike; if the pitcher throws four balls, you have achieved your purpose.
- Don't be afraid to bunt on 1-1 or 2-1. The infielders will probably have moved back a little and will be more apt to look for you to swing away.
- Stay relaxed when you get the bunt sign. Remember, you have practiced long hours and are prepared to lay down a perfect bunt.
- To become a good bunter, you must overcome any fear of the ball.
- Try not to make it obvious that you're checking the third baseman's position. The infielders will pick up on that quickly.
- Bunt the ball and *then* run. Location is more important than jumping out of the box.
- Practice will provide the confidence you need to become an excellent bunter.
- You must have the desire to become a good bunter.
- Realize the enormous mental pressure you can put on the defense with a great bunt.
- Practice bunting and use it in the games. Always remember: You'll lose it if you don't use it.

DRILLS

Sacrifice Bunt Drill

PURPOSE: To teach a player to bunt a ball in the correct area.

EQUIPMENT: Field, baseballs, bats, cones

IMPLEMENTATION:

1. Mark off two lines 5 to 10 feet away from home plate. Cones or balls can be used to mark off a certain area.
2. Set up a pitcher and catcher, and place one player on each of the baselines to retrieve bunted balls (shaggers).
3. Have each player work on the techniques of the sacrifice bunt, trying to bunt the ball into the designated areas. Have each player bunt the ball to both sides several times.
4. Players can also work on getting the ball to stop in the designated areas by deadening the ball with the proper technique.

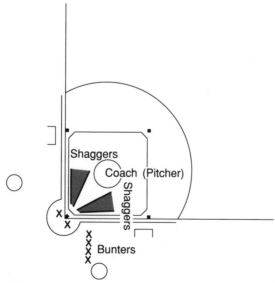

Figure 2.16

Game Variation

IMPLEMENTATION:

1. Divide the players into two teams for a 30-minute drill.
2. Designate certain areas into which players are to bunt the ball.
3. Give each player one chance to bunt the ball into those areas.
4. Record the number of correctly bunted balls.

Bunting for a Hit Drill

PURPOSE: To teach players to base hit.

EQUIPMENT: Balls, bats, infield, pitching machine

IMPLEMENTATION:

1. Set up a pitching machine just in front of the pitcher's mound about 45 feet away from home plate, and set up infielders at each position.
2. Have a coach feed the balls, with a catcher at home plate.
3. Have the hitter assume his normal stance and show bunt only after the ball has been thrown.
4. Have the hitter work on bunting the ball in the designated areas.
5. Have the bunter get the ball down and then take one cross-over step toward first base.

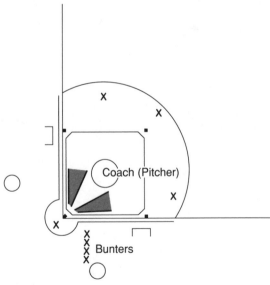

Figure 2.17

Game Variation

IMPLEMENTATION:

1. Divide the players into two teams.
2. Have one team play the field while the other team bunts.
3. Play a game in which the players are allowed only to bunt.
4. Do not allow the defense to break until the hitter shows bunt. Have a coach check for early breaks.

CHAPTER 3

Getting to
First Base

The most obvious—and most important—truism in baseball is, "The team that scores more runs wins."

Notice: not better coaching, not more hits, not fewer errors, not better players, but *more runs*.

And it doesn't make any difference how you score the runs—three singles, a home run, walks, errors, and so on. A run is a run is a run.

Teams that have trouble with the bat—and that includes most high school and college teams—have to try another route. They have to do it with their feet and their wits, which means intelligent baserunning—getting the most out of your limited offensive weapons. Aggressive baserunning will often make the defense worry and hurry, and this will definitely give the edge to the offense.

All baserunning has to start in the dugout. In short, the player must start doing his homework before he ever gets to bat or reaches first base.

While sitting or standing in the dugout, he should study the opposing pitcher intently, looking for an edge.

- What kind of pickoff move does the pitcher have?
- Is the pitcher locating his pitches?
- Does he have a great breaking pitch?
- What pitch does he go to in a jam?
- Does he tip off his delivery by the way he holds the ball in his glove?
- Does he cock his head or his hip or his arm in a certain way when he throws a fastball or breaking ball?
- Does he have more than one way to throw to first—a "calling card" move (just to let the runner know that he is watching him) and a quick, deceitful, "best" move?

The intelligent base runner will want to know everything possible—every idiosyncrasy—about the pitcher. Something he does every time he throws to first or to the plate. Anything that will give the base runner an edge.

Also consider the third baseman. Is he playing too deep? Can you bunt on him? Any of these "little things" can give the alert base runner an edge, which is all a good base runner needs to get the extra base. That can score runs and steal ball games.

ON-DECK CIRCLE

The player should continue to study the pitcher and defense as he prepares to come to the plate. He should use this time to swing a loaded bat, fungo bat, or regular bat to get loose. He can also work on timing the pitcher by triggering his bat and taking a short step in time with the pitching delivery.

With a runner in scoring position, the on-deck hitter should keep alert for a play at the plate. He must become a coach for anyone attempting to score on a close play.

By positioning himself directly in line with third base and home, he can signal the runner to slide or stand up. He can also clear the area of loose equipment, such as a bat or catcher's mask, that may hold up the base runner or cause an injury.

BATTER'S BOX

With a runner on second, the hitter must check the runner to see whether he's trying to relay any information to him. Most runners can pick up the catcher's signs from second base, and he should have some kind of system to relay the pitch to the hitter. For example, if the base runner at second takes his lead bending over, a curveball is coming. If he is standing more erect, then the pitcher is going to throw a fastball.

Whenever the pitcher throws over to first base, the batter should step out of the box to give the runner a chance to reestablish his lead, particularly in a steal situation. This will keep the pitcher from quick pitching and keeping the runner off guard.

The batter must also be on the alert for wild pitches and passed balls. Runners don't always see the play clearly, and it's up to the hitter to advise the runners to advance to the next base or to hold up. This is particularly important with a runner on third.

As you can see, baserunning begins way before the ball is hit.

GOING FROM HOME TO FIRST

The running begins the moment the batter contacts the ball. He must get out of the box as quickly and efficiently as possible. That is the key to a good jump.

Running efficiency goes hand in hand with good batting mechanics. The batter who hits off his heels or is otherwise off balance is going to have difficulty getting a good jump. Other common mistakes include watching the ball after it leaves the bat, instead of concentrating on the jump, and standing up instead of staying low.

You want the hitter to stay low and drive out of the box with a jab step with the back foot. If necessary, the batter may have to take a short cross-over step with the rear foot. The step with the back foot ensures the quickest and most efficient (balanced) way to come out of the batter's box.

On his third step, the player must locate the ball—see whether it went through the infield or was caught or knocked down. He must do this with a quick look, not a stare. Staring is a time killer that will slow the runner down. The quick glance is a more positive action. It lets the runner know whether to run through the bag or make his turn at first.

Ground Ball in the Infield

In running down the line on a ball hit to the infield, the runner should fix his eyes on a point about 10 yards beyond the bag. He should never consider the base the end of the line, because that might cause him to slow down. He must also avoid looking down, because this may cause him to run off-line.

COACHING POINT

I like our players to fix their eyes on the outfield grass, because this will tend to make them go hard through the base.

As shown in Figure 3.1, the player must run like a sprinter with his head up, body leaning forward, arms pumping front to back (not across the chest), and feet moving in a straight line. Unless he believes there's a chance of advancing, he must run right through the bag.

It's also the runner's responsibility to locate the ball in case it's thrown away. It's easier for the runner to do this than for the coach to locate the overthrow and then relay the message to the runner.

Figure 3.1

The runner, while approaching first, should observe the first baseman's feet. If he sees the first baseman coming down the line to field the ball, he should move to the foul side of the baseline and hit the dirt to avoid a tag. The runner who watches the movement of the first baseman will avoid collisions and tags.

Ground Ball Through the Infield

Once the runner sees the ball going through the infield, he should concentrate on making an aggressive turn at first. He must pressure the defense to come up with the ball as quickly as possible.

It is best to veer out on about the third step and to run toward first base on a path no more than 3 or 4 feet outside the line (see Figure 3.2).

COACHING POINT

The veer really depends on the runner—his build, size, and agility. Some runners may have to veer out sooner; others may be able to wait a little longer. You may find that a bigger player will have to veer out sooner than a smaller player, who is likely to be more agile.

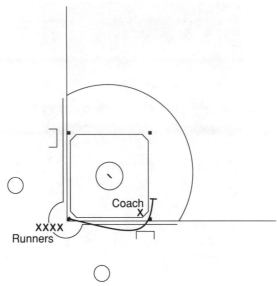

Figure 3.2

The runner should hit the left inside corner of the bag with his left foot and get a good push-off to second, leaning in and cutting the bag sharply. If touching the bag with his left foot will cause him to break stride, the runner should, of course, touch the base with the other foot—whatever feels most comfortable and efficient to him.

The key to making an aggressive turn and going on a straight line to second is dipping the left shoulder and leaning the upper body toward the inside of the infield (Figure 3.3).

The runner who loafs on his way from home to first will lose his double, triple, or inside-the-parker.

The length of the turn is based on the location of the ball. If the ball is hit to right field, the runner cannot take as big a turn as he could on a hit to left field.

When returning to the bag after a single, the runner should never take his eyes off the ball. He should look over his shoulder while hustling back to first. If the ball is hit to the center fielder's left, the runner should turn his left shoulder toward the right-field side of the diamond. If the ball is hit to the center fielder, or to the right of the center fielder, the runner should turn his right shoulder toward the infield side of the diamond.

Figure 3.3

If the outfielder makes a habit of throwing behind runners as they turn the bag, a smart runner can go as soon as the fielder lets go of the ball. The runner must be careful, however. On a ball hit to right field, the catcher may be covering first. So the runner cannot afford to wander too far.

GOING FOR TWO

During the opponent's pregame drills, the heads-up base runner will check the outfielders' arms. The outfielder with an average to weak arm will be vulnerable on balls hit to the gaps. The smart base runner will always take the extra base on a gapper. On a ball in the gap, the outfielder will have trouble catching the ball, planting his feet, and then getting off a strike to second base in time.

If the outfielder loafs after a ball, the runner will make him pay for it by turning the bag and going on. The outfielder who carelessly lobs the ball in to the cutoff man can be made to pay the price in the same fashion. The runner will never pause at first but will just keep on going. A great time to try this is with two outs.

Even when outfielders hustle to the ball, a base runner can sometimes take the extra base on him. How many times do you see an outfielder throw the ball directly to second on-line?

COACHING POINT

Going for two is not a bad gamble with two outs, especially against an outfielder with just an average arm. But it is not a good play when your team is down three or four runs and trying to get back into the game.

Runners in scoring position must always read the throws going to third and home from the outfielders. Whenever a lead runner is advancing to the next base and the outfielder overthrows the cutoff man, the back runner should immediately head for second base.

It is sometimes easy to read the ball out of the outfielder's hand. The runner who concentrates on reading the trajectory of the throw will wind up with a lot of gift packages. If the ball leaves the outfielder's hand with a high trajectory, the base runner knows that the ball will go over the cutoff man's head.

Coaches may be furious with the unalert base runner who stands on first on such overthrows. Now you have first and third, perhaps one out, and the next hitter grounds into a double play. Result: Instead of your team having two outs and one run in, the inning's over. This is a prime example of why intelligent baserunning wins ball games.

When a runner takes advantage of a bad throw and advances to second, you can count on the defense feeling the mental breakdown. A few more mistakes and they are mentally defeated.

Every smart, aggressive high school and college team will win games in which they get only three or four hits, but scored a few runs. How? Intelligent baserunning.

Mental Aspects for Players

Have your players keep the following ideas in mind:

- In the dugout, always be looking for an edge over the defense.

- You don't have to reach first base to learn the pitcher's best move. You can pick it up from the dugout.
- After you detect a pitcher's idiosyncrasy, focus all your attention on it.
- Check the playing field to see if the grass is wet or the grass is high (in the event of a bunt).
- Study the outfielders' arms in pre-infield practice.
- See if the catcher sets up a certain way for a fastball, a curveball, and so on.
- Study the pitcher to see if he is developing a pattern on his pitch selection. This can be of great help when you reach first base and are thinking of stealing.
- Always be aware of the (dirt) surface around first base. If it is sandy, call time out and clean it out.
- Don't allow the pitcher to quick-pitch you as you're taking your lead.
- When you get your 10- to 12-foot lead, make sure you feel you're only 3 feet off the base. The lead must be a comfortable, safe one.
- Program your mind to steal—think positive.
- Once you start worrying about being picked off, you will never get a good jump. Don't think negative.
- If you get picked off, don't brood about it. Everyone gets picked off once in a while. Learn from it.

DRILLS

Down-the-Line Drill

PURPOSE: To teach players the proper mechanics in running down the line.

EQUIPMENT: Infield from home plate to first base

IMPLEMENTATION:

1. Have players line up at home plate.
2. Place a coach in the infield grass between third base and shortstop.
3. Have each player simulate a swing, cross over out of the box, and head down the line toward first base.
4. On his third step, have him glance in toward the coach. If the coach is holding up one arm, the runner runs through the base.
5. On the next runner, have the coach hold up two arms. This tells the runner to veer out because the ball went through the infield.
6. The coach can alternate signals to keep the runners honest.
7. Key: Have the runners glance, not stare, when they look in at the coach.

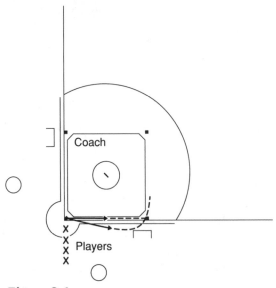

Figure 3.4

Advancing to Second Base Drill

PURPOSE: To teach players the proper mechanics in taking the extra base. This drill enables the runner to read the ball and determine the plays in which he can advance to second. This is also an excellent drill in which the outfielders can work on their offensive skills.

EQUIPMENT: Fungo bats, baseballs, helmets

IMPLEMENTATION:

1. Have several players line up at home, each wearing a helmet.
2. Have nine players take the field after loosening up their arms.
3. Place a coach at home with a fungo bat and plenty of baseballs.
4. Have the coach ground the ball into the outfield, and have the runner round first base and read the outfielder.
5. If the runner thinks he can advance, he continues to second base.

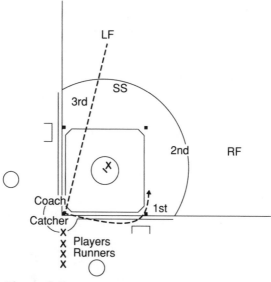

Figure 3.5

CHAPTER 4

Reading the Pitcher for Giveaways

Pitchers are creatures of habit. Almost all of them have some idiosyncrasy in their motion—something they do all the time without knowing it. The quirk may be harmless, or it may be extremely meaningful. That is why every intelligent ball club will put the opposing pitcher under a microscope, constantly studying him from the dugout, the on-deck circle, and the bases, checking every body part to discover exactly what he does when he throws to first base or delivers to the plate.

Both the players and the coaches look for a giveaway—a telltale sign that will enable the runner to get a good jump and maybe steal a base . . . steal a run . . . maybe even steal the ball game. He's looking for *the edge*.

The first runner to reach base plays a vital role in this cat-and-mouse game. He is trained to take a good one-way lead and then begin enticing the pitcher to throw over . . . once, twice, maybe three times.

He wants the pitcher to show his best move. Every experienced pitcher has this kind of move, and the runner must look for it. The runner must discern between the "calling card" move—the perfunctory throw-over that delivers the simple message, "I'm watching you"—and the "move" that is definitely designed to pick him off.

The runner must keep on his toes, ready to dart back each time the pitcher throws over. Intelligent reading and quick reactions will enable a team to run against both right-handed and left-handed pitchers.

COACHING POINT

If the pitcher has an excellent move, he is going to use it. If he has a poor move, he is seldom going to throw over.

FOCAL POINTS WITH RIGHT-HANDED PITCHERS

Following are the eight major checkpoints a runner must look for in reading a right-handed pitcher. Remember, with a runner on first, the pitcher will be working from a stretch position; in throwing to first or delivering to the plate, he will have to flex his knees and move his heels.

Lifting Right Heel vs. Lifting Left Heel

This is the easiest focal point for the runner.

When the right-handed pitcher throws to first, he will lift his *right* heel to clear the rubber (see Figure 4.1a).

When the pitcher delivers to the plate, he will lift his *left* heel to pick up his foot (see Figure 4.1b).

The smart runner will react accordingly. If the left heel lifts—go! If it opens up—back!

Figure 4.1a   b

Cap Bill Pointing Down vs. Cap Bill Pointing Up

The right-handed pitcher will tilt his head down and a little to his left to check the runner out of the corner of his (left) eye.

When he throws over to first, he will turn his head and keep the cap bill *down* (see Figure 4.2a).

When he throws to home plate, he will lift his head so that his cap bill will point *up* as he kicks and delivers (check Figure 4.2b).

Figure 4.2a   b

Open Shoulder vs. Closed Shoulder

Many pitchers will come set with their left shoulder open to get a clear view of the runner. The open shoulder will, however, increase the pitcher's vulnerability to a steal. When he goes to the plate, he will have to turn the shoulder in (toward the plate). As soon as that shoulder moves, the runner can go (Figure 4.3)!

Figure 4.3a   **b**   **c**

The base runner's key is obviously as follows: Watch the pitcher's left shoulder. If it opens up, he is going to first. If he turns the shoulder in, he is going to the plate. The balk rule protects the runner. It forbids the pitcher to close his shoulder and then go to first. That is a balk.

The Front Elbow

This presents another potential giveaway. As the right-hander comes to his set position, he will bring his elbow close to his body. His first move from that position will tip off his intention.

If he decides to throw over to first, he will swing his front elbow in that direction (Figure 4.4).

If he decides to go to the plate, he will simply bring the elbow up in his natural motion (Figure 4.5).

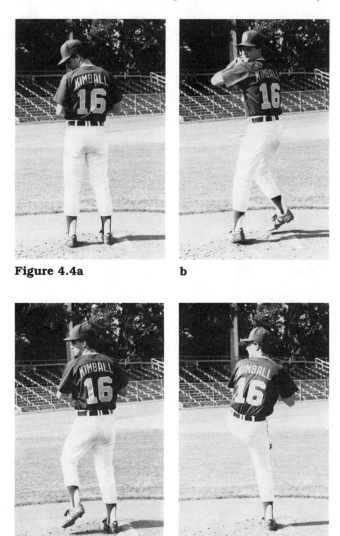

Figure 4.4a   b

Figure 4.5a   b

The runner has the edge. He's able to see the elbow lift away from the body and also detect the gap ("daylight") between the elbow and the body.

Shoulder Lean

Some pitchers start leaning toward the plate before picking up the front foot. Leaning is a fatal flaw. As soon as the

Figure 4.6a   b

runner detects the front shoulder moving toward the plate, he can be off for second (Figure 4.6).

Head Position

Some pitchers will always look toward third base before throwing to first. Then, if they want to go to the plate, they will look home. This gives the runner the added confidence of knowing when the pitcher is trying to pick him off (Figure 4.7).

Figure 4.7a   b

Rhythm Pitcher

Right-handers tend to develop a certain rhythm in coming set, checking the runner, and delivering to the plate. It is an easy thing to detect and, subsequently, exploit.

The reading must be done from the dugout. The coach and/or the players can "count" out the pitcher—that is, count 1, 2, or 3 seconds to see how long it takes the pitcher to kick and go to the plate from his set position.

Throwing From the Top

The pitcher who throws strictly from the top of his stretch is also easy to read and steal on. Once he comes set, he'll go home 90 percent of the time. The runner should wait until the pitcher comes set and, as he reaches the top of his set, go (Figure 4.8)!

Figure 4.8

FOCAL POINTS WITH LEFT-HANDED PITCHERS

Because most pitchers are right-handed, most base runners have trouble dealing with left-handers—first, because they don't see that many left-handed pitchers, and second, because the left-hander has a definite advantage over the runner on first. In his stretch position, he has a straight-on view of the runner at first.

Nevertheless, many left-handers are comparatively easy to run on. Intelligent reading and good reactions will enable the runner to run against the left-handed pitcher just as easily as against the right-hander. The runner can check the southpaw pitcher for 10 giveaways:

Pitcher Who Looks at First vs. Pitcher Who Looks Home

Many left-handers try to deceive the runner by always looking away from their target. For example, when delivering to the plate, the left-hander may look toward first as he kicks to keep the runner close. Check Figure 4.9.

Figure 4.9a   b

Conversely, when throwing to first, the left-hander will turn his head toward home to fake the runner into thinking he is going to the plate. See Figure 4.10 for the famous, maybe slightly notorious, left-hander's "balk move."

The pitcher may also move his head from first to home several times in trying to confuse the runner. This kind of pitcher will often give away his intent with his final look. For example, if the pitcher looks at first when he kicks, he will be throwing home. If he looks toward home, he will be going to first base. This is one of the easiest moves to detect, and most left-hander pitchers are addicted to it.

Figure 4.10a   b

High Leg Kick vs. Low Leg Kick

The pitcher will use a low kick when going to first to get a better angle for his throw (see Figure 4.11). When he goes to the plate, he will kick higher (Figure 4.12).

A smart base runner will be able to pick up the difference and use it to his advantage.

Figure 4.11a   b

Figure 4.12a   b

Erect Upper Body vs. Arched Upper Body

When throwing to first, the pitcher will tilt his upper body (Figure 4.13). When delivering to the plate, he will keep his torso more erect (Figure 4.14).

Figure 4.13a   b

Figure 4.14a   b

Toe Position

The direction in which the pitcher points his lead foot offers another good cue for the runner.

When throwing to the plate, many left-handers tend to point the toe *up*, allowing the runner to see the sole of the foot. Check Figure 4.15a.

When throwing to first base, the pitcher will point his toe *down* (Figure 4.15b). The runner should concentrate on the lead foot and react accordingly.

Figure 4.15a   b

Breaking the Plane of the Rubber

The plane of the rubber is an imaginary line running from the back edge of the rubber to first base. Whenever any part of the left-hander's right leg, foot, or knee breaks this line, he must go to the plate.

Many left-handers will "break the plane" to get a little extra on the pitch. An observant base runner will pick this up and get a good jump. Figure 4.16 offers an excellent example of a left-hander breaking the imaginary plane. He cannot do this (break the plane) on a throw to first. It will be called a balk.

Figure 4.16a   **b**

Most of the time the pitcher will kick up slowly, without breaking the plane, on a throw to first. Figure 4.17 shows the pitcher kicking up from the set position and throwing to first base.

Gap Between the Legs

The left-hander will often kick out slightly toward the first-base line to get a better angle on his throw to first base. Some left-handers will also do this to deceive the runner. In any case, they will leave a wider space between the pivot leg and the stride leg on the kick (Figure 4.18).

Figure 4.17a   **b**

Figure 4.18

When going to the plate, the pitcher will use a more closed kick to obtain more push from the rubber (Figure 4.19). The runner must concentrate on the gap and can be off and running if the kick stays closed.

Figure 4.19

Hands Higher vs. Hands Lower

Some pitchers will lift their hands higher when they throw to first base (Figure 4.20) and will keep their hands a little lower and tend to bring them back more when they deliver to the plate (Figure 4.21).

Figure 4.20a   **b**

Figure 4.21

Quick Kick vs. Slow Kick

Many left-handers will use a slow kick and open their legs when going to first and use a quicker and more closed kick when delivering to the plate.

Many runners freeze or stutter-step on the quick kick. The smart runner will anticipate the quick kick and break for second on it.

Big Lead vs. Short Lead

One of the best ways to steal on a left-hander is to set him up with a big lead (15 feet). As soon as the pitcher kicks, the runner should dart back to first. He should then shorten up his lead to convince the pitcher that he isn't going anywhere.

On the pitcher's next move, the runner should *go*! He should keep going even if the pitcher throws over to first. It will take two throws, two catches, and a tag to get the runner out. The left-handed pitcher will seldom throw over more than twice unless he has an outstanding move.

Even though the plan is somewhat of a gamble, it often works. The only exception would be on a quick throw to first. The runner should then get into a rundown and try to get back to first (or wind up on second).

Shoulders

The runner can get a good jump by concentrating on the pitcher's shoulder. When throwing to the plate, the pitcher will keep his shoulders squared to the runner (on first) (Figure 4.22). When throwing to first, he will turn his front shoulder toward the bag to put something on his throw (Figure 4.23).

Figure 4.22a   b

Figure 4.23a   b

Mental Aspects for Players

Instruct your players to keep the following points in mind:

- The runner must do his homework before he reaches first base. While in the dugout, he should study the pitcher and try to determine his best move.
- The runner must concentrate on the positive—getting a good lead—rather than on the negative—worrying about getting picked off.
- Determine whether the pitcher has a quick pickoff move or a slow one.
- Determine whether the pitcher has a slow kick to the plate.
- Determine whether the catcher has a good release time (2.0 to 2.1 seconds).
- Determine whether the pitcher has both a slow pickoff move and a quick pickoff move.
- Make sure that runners secure a 10- to 12-foot stealing lead.
- Runners should concentrate their efforts and thoughts on the jump rather than on not getting picked off.
- Runners must learn to go from the back edge of first base to the back edge of second base.
- The shortest distance between two points will always be a straight line.

DRILLS

Reading Pitcher's Moves Drill I

PURPOSE: To teach players visual concentration on a certain body part idiosyncrasy of the pitcher. This drill forces the player to *concentrate* entirely on the pitcher's move.

EQUIPMENT: Grassy area in the outfield or first-base area of the infield

IMPLEMENTATION:

1. Have three lines of four players each assume a stealing lead off first base.
2. Put a coach on the mound and have him demonstrate certain movements of the head, shoulder, and so forth.
3. Now have the coach go through the moves while the players (without moving) yell out each move. After their verbal read, have them go back to the bag.

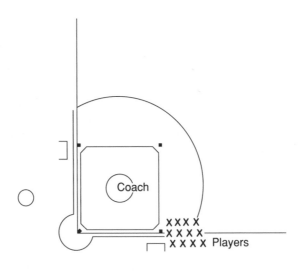

Figure 4.24

Reading Pitcher's Moves Drill II

PURPOSE: To teach players the proper technique of reading a pitcher's move and getting a good jump. This drill enables the player to see the "pitcher's" move and then break in the correct direction, giving him confidence in reading and getting the best possible jump.

EQUIPMENT: Grassy area in the outfield or first-base area of the infield

IMPLEMENTATION:

1. Have the players assume a stealing lead (off first) in three even lines.
2. Put a coach on the mound and have him demonstrate certain head and shoulder movements.
3. This time, have the players yell "back" or "go," and, at the same time, cross over accordingly (cross toward second or cross back to the bag).
4. Have the players take only two steps in either direction.

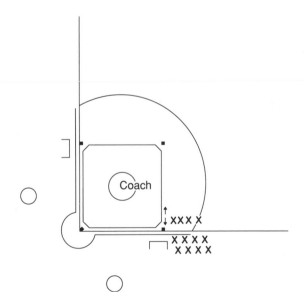

Figure 4.25

CHAPTER 5

Aggressive Running From First to Second

*B*ack in the 1960s, inspired by Maury Wills, base-ball experienced a renaissance on every level because of baserunning. The base runners started taking the extra base and looking for the steal, and this made for a more exciting and potent offense.

Players found this kind of play quick, exciting, and psychologically stimulating, which gave the offense an aggressive edge.

On the high school and college levels, running has always been a way of life. With players' hitting, throwing, and fielding skills and playing surfaces usually leaving much to be desired, it has obviously paid to run.

RUNNING AGAINST THE CLOCK

One of the best ways to improve a team's baserunning is by timing the opposing battery.

College and high school pitchers are taught to deliver quickly from the set position, registering from 1.3 to 1.5 seconds on the fastball and from 1.5 to 1.8 seconds on the curveball or change-up. Timing is measured from the pitcher's first movement to when the ball hits the catcher's mitt. Pitchers with a high leg kick will register poor times.

Catchers should be able to deliver the ball to second base in 1.9 to 2.3 seconds from the time the ball hits the mitt until the ball is caught at second base.

So, we can calculate the total time of the pitch and throw to second as follows:

- *Fastball* (1.3 to 1.5 seconds) and catcher's throw (1.9 to 2.3 seconds) = range of 3.2 to 3.8 seconds
- *Curveball* (1.5 to 1.8 seconds) and catcher's throw (1.9 to 2.3 seconds) = range of 3.4 to 4.1 seconds

In short, the base runner, to be consistently successful, must be able to take off and arrive at second base in 3.5 seconds or less.

COACHING POINT

The coach should time every base runner. If he times out the opposing battery at 3.5 to 3.7 seconds for the fastball and between 3.8 and 4.0 seconds for the curveball, he can expect his base runners to steal bases without any problems as long as their times are between 3.3 and 3.6 seconds.

"Making something happen" via the steal can cause even a well-coached team to panic as it applies pressure to the defense. Actually, your team will cause the defense to make unnecessary errors because of the mental pressure that you have applied. The opposing pitcher will lose his concentration and composure; the infielders will move toward the bag too soon, leaving holes in the infield; catchers will start to call more fastballs and pitchouts; managers will put on more pickoff plays.

All of this can swing the momentum toward the aggressive running team.

STEALING SECOND BASE

The good base stealer is rarely "born" or "found." He is developed. Great speed is not a prerequisite. It can certainly help, but it isn't imperative.

During my coaching years at Florida State, and now at Tennessee, some of the best base stealers have possessed only average speed. Their chief asset was quickness of mind in deciding when or when not to go.

Primary Lead

The art of stealing begins with the primary lead at first base.

The length of the lead depends on the player. Factors that affect his lead include lateral quickness, condition of the field, quickness of the pitcher's pickoff move, importance of the run, and whether the runner is stealing or just reading the pitcher for a pitch or two.

The runner should get between a 10- and a 12-foot lead. The important thing is that he feels comfortable and safe with the lead. The runner should know that he can dive back safely. The runner who gets a big 12-foot lead and then becomes too concerned about getting picked off isn't going to get a good jump. He'd do better to get a 10-foot lead and feel comfortable. I tell runners to feel as though they are only 2 feet off the base.

If they have done their homework, they won't have to be concerned about getting picked off. Note: It's up to the runner to decide how far off base to get. Remember, somewhere between 10 and 12 feet is adequate.

Before taking his lead, the runner must do three things:

1. Check for the number of outs
2. Check the coach for a sign
3. Check the defense for alignment

Figure 5.1 shows how the runner places both heels on the corners of the base as he checks the three points.

Figure 5.1

The runner accomplishes the primary lead by taking two long cross-over steps followed by two or three shuffle steps. The runner steps with his right foot first, then his left. After the second step, he must immediately turn to face the pitcher and take his shuffle steps.

This method of taking the primary lead will let the player know exactly how far off the base he is. Each cross-over step will take him about 3 feet off, and each shuffle step will add about 2 feet. In short, two cross-over steps and two shuffle steps will bring him approximately 10 feet off the base, and a third shuffle step will make it about 12 feet. See Figure 5.2.

Figure 5.2a   b   c

d   e

This kind of calculation will eliminate the need for the runner to look back and will ensure a consistent lead. Think about this: How many times have you seen a runner get picked off while he's looking back to find the base?

COACHING POINT

The runner should always remember that the shortest distance between two points is a straight line. He should avoid edging 1 or 2 feet behind or in front of the straight line. This will cause him to run an extra step or two, which can cost him on a close play. Why run 82 or 83 feet (after taking a 10-foot lead) instead of just 80?

Some coaches have their runner lead off the front edge of the bag, putting him one or two feet in front. The hope is that this will present an optical illusion to the pitcher, making him think that the runner isn't as far off the base as he actually is. The disadvantage is that the runner's angle of return on a pickoff may carry him into the tag. Also, as previously discussed, it may cause him to run an extra step or two on the way to second.

I tell a runner to take his lead just off the back corner of the base. This will make him a tougher tag on a pickoff attempt. The first baseman will now have to reach for him (see Figure 5.3).

I teach the runner to go from the back corner of first to the back (right-field) corner of second on a straight line and to reach for the bag with his left hand, which makes him a tough tag for the middle infielder.

As the runner takes his lead, I want him to train his eyes on the pitcher, staying low in a good position to dive back on a pickoff. The runner should take his lead while the pitcher is getting his sign and should avoid moving while the pitcher is going to the set position. A lot of pitchers like to throw over when going to the set position.

Stance

Upon reaching his maximum stealing lead, the runner should be in a good running stance: feet shoulder-width apart, knees slightly bent, arms flexed in front, weight on the balls of the feet, upper body at a 45-degree angle (Figure 5.4).

Some players like to stand more erect, whereas others like to stay lower to the ground. Usually taller players will stand a little higher than shorter players.

Figure 5.3a

b

c

d

Figure 5.4

The right foot should be opened and dropped back a little, with the right toes on line with the left instep, allowing the runner to pivot on the right toe and push off straight for second base. A toe-to-toe alignment would force the runner to take a short step left of the straight line as he crosses over. Remember, every 10th of a second counts.

Arms

Most runners either fail to get the most out of their arms or use the wrong arm action. They usually let their arms hang loose and then raise them as they cross over. This is wasted motion.

The runner should get his arms out in front, flexed. As he pivots on his right foot, he should drive his left arm toward second in an uppercutting fashion and then pull it back. At the same time, he should throw his right arm back toward first.

In essence, he must pump his arms like a sprinter coming out of the blocks—except that he pivots on his right foot and crosses over with his left. And, just like a sprinter, he must stay low as he crosses over (Figure 5.5)—not rise up, as this would slow him down. He should start low to the ground and gradually rise up on each stride.

When referring to this action, I use the term "get the money and run." Former big leaguer Joe Pitman of the Houston Astros told me about a drill for improving this skill. One player gets in a running position while the other

Figure 5.5a   **b**

holds a batting glove in front of him. The runner must snatch the glove as he runs past the other player, starting in a low position and rising up some on each stride. See the Cross-Over Drill at the end of this chapter.

One-Way Lead

This commits the runner to cross over back to first or to go to second on the first movement of the pitcher from his set position.

As a rule, the first runner to reach first assumes a one-way lead and entices the pitcher to throw over. The runner moves several feet farther from the base than he normally would. The length of the lead (about 15 feet) will cause the pitcher to throw over—and give away his pickoff move. The runner must break back to the bag at the pitcher's first movement, regardless of where he throws the ball.

When a steal is in order, the runner must break for second on the pitcher's first move, no matter where he goes.

Two-Way Lead

This lead is used when the runner must read the pitcher and react accordingly. The runner's weight is over the balls of the feet, and he is now ready to go in either direction.

Walking Lead

The runner moves out and never comes to a dead stop. He keeps taking steps and slides, which enables him to get a great jump. This allows him to be more effective than he would be if taking off from a dead stop. (This lead is particularly effective at second base, because it is very difficult to steal third from a dead stop.)

Secondary Lead

The purpose of the secondary lead is to reduce the distance between the bases; it enables the runner to eat up ground as the pitcher goes to the plate from the set position. Of course, this kind of lead is used in a non-steal situation.

The idea is to extend the primary lead with two shuffle steps as the pitcher kicks and throws to the plate. The runner, on his second shuffle step, should land on his right foot at about the same time that the ball reaches the hitting area. If the ball is hit, the runner must read the contact (line drive/ground ball). If it is a hit, he can pivot on his right foot, cross over, and head for second without stopping. If the ball is caught by the catcher, the runner can simply push off the already-planted right foot and return to first.

The key to avoiding a pickoff attempt is to take two quick cross-over steps back to first. The runner who drops his head and lackadaisically returns to first is a prime candidate to be picked off.

RETURNING TO FIRST

It is essential for a runner to know how to return to first base quickly and safely.

Although the first-base coach can help, it's the runner's responsibility to read the pitcher and react to the pickoff throw. The runner cannot rely wholly on the first-base coach, because the ball will have already been released by the time he can react to the coach's command.

Factors that determine whether the runner should return to first standing or diving include the following:

- The length of the lead when the pitcher throws to first
- Whether the runner is stealing or not
- The quickness of the pitcher's pickoff move
- The field conditions

Returning to First Standing

When at all possible, I want our runner to dive back. If, however, the pitcher has a slow move or a soft toss, or if

Figure 5.6a

b

c

d

the runner is only a few feet off the base, he'll often be able to return standing up.

In Figure 5.6, the runner returns to first base with a crossover of the right foot, a left step, and another crossover with the right foot, landing on the inside front part of the base. This method protects the runner, is quick, and allows the runner to quickly advance on a wild throw. It also prevents the first baseman from reaching out for a wild throw to his right. You can see how difficult it would be for a first baseman to catch a wild throw, especially down low to the ground, to his right.

COACHING POINT

Some runners like to return by touching the base with the left foot and spinning away from the tag. The risk lies in coming off the base. The runner also becomes vulnerable to a wild throw.

Returning to First Diving

This is the quickest and most aggressive way to return to first on a pickoff attempt.

The technique is simple. The runner pivots on his left foot while crossing over hard with his right. He slides hard (on his chest) into the bag, extending his right arm toward the back corner.

His hand should hit the ground away from the base to avoid jamming the shoulder. He must point his fingers up and keep his head up to check for bad throws that can enable him to advance. See Figure 5.7.

DELAYED STEAL

Although every base runner cannot be a threat to run, he can take advantage of a sleeping defense. The delayed steal offers a way for anyone to steal a base.

Whereas the normal secondary lead consists of two shuffle steps from the primary lead, the delayed steal usually requires three shuffle steps.

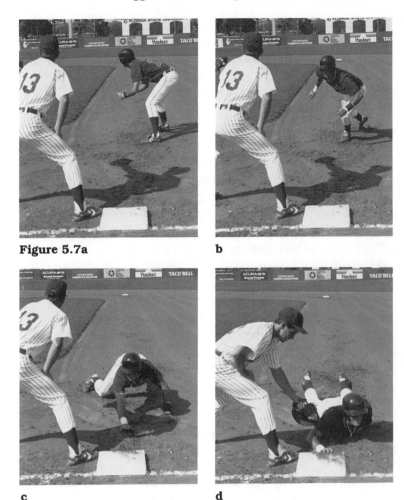

Figure 5.7a   b

c   d

COACHING POINT

The runner must make his three-shuffle-step lead look the same as the double shuffle in his normal secondary lead.

The runner starts with a normal (primary) lead, then extends his lead with three or four shuffle steps (secondary lead) after the pitcher delivers to the plate. He will then add a third shuffle step, coming down on the right foot as the catcher takes the pitch. He will then pivot on this foot, cross over with the left, and go. Some players will need four quick shuffle steps before the ball hits the catcher's mitt. The key is to shuffle until the ball hits the mitt.

As the word "shuffle" implies, the feet do not cross in the execution of the lead. The runner, bent over with knees flexed, facing the inside of the diamond, steps laterally with his right foot, then shuffles his left foot over and hops with his right. He then steps laterally with his right foot and repeats the shuffle.

That gives him his normal (double shuffle) secondary lead. Whenever the setup is right for the delayed steal, he will take a third or fourth shuffle step, making sure not to exaggerate any of his moves or do anything else that would catch the defense's eye and give away the steal. Remember, it is essential that the runner not cross over until the ball hits the catcher's mitt.

Timing is of the essence. The runner must come down on his right foot as the catcher receives the ball. He does not want to be caught during or between shuffles, because that would set him up for a pickoff throw.

If the middle infielders or the catcher are not paying attention, the runner can go as his right foot comes down after the third shuffle. As on a regular steal, he must pivot on his front (right) foot and cross over hard with his left foot, letting his momentum drive his body straight for second.

Defense Against a Delayed Steal

A word about the defense against a delayed steal: A smart shortstop will check the runner (at first) after the pitch is taken by the catcher. This quick glance will let the infielder know what the runner is doing.

Figure 5.8 shows what the catcher can do to safeguard against a delayed steal. Upon catching the ball, he will immediately prepare to throw to second. An alert infield (catcher and middle infielders) will take away the opportunity for a delayed steal.

Defensive Mistakes

Now let's look at some of the defensive mistakes that lead to offensive success: (1) the infielders start to get tired,

Figure 5.8a

b

c

especially when a pitcher is walking people; and (2) the defense, down by four or five runs early in the game, starts to get sloppy.

This is when you find the middle infielders looking down or away after a pitch instead of checking the runner at first.

The catcher can also become lazy and indifferent as he catches the ball. If the catcher receives the ball and then falls to his knees, he will allow the smart base runner to advance to the next base.

This kind of thing can also happen when the catcher tries to frame the pitch. Inexperienced catchers tend to worry more about framing the pitch than watching the runner. Result: They don't move into a throwing position quickly enough to nail a stealer.

The sleeping middle infielder or catcher is going to allow the offense to steal a lot of bases. Even if the catcher is alert, the runner will have at least a 90 percent chance of stealing against middle infielders who are looking at the ground. The catcher simply won't have anyone to throw to.

Conversely, an alert shortstop isn't going to be of much help if the catcher drops to his knees. By the time the catcher sees the runner advancing, it will be too late to rise and throw to second.

During the game, it is important for the coaches to observe the tendencies of the middle infielders and the catcher.

- Do they look at the ground?
- Does the catcher drop to his knees after he receives the ball?
- Does the catcher take too long to frame the pitch?

Typical Delayed-Steal Play

After a pitch, the shortstop looks down at the ground. The catcher is alert but has no one to throw to.

As I have said, the trick lies in the runner taking the secondary lead with three surreptitious shuffle steps instead of two. Anyone who can do this is a threat to steal. Johnny Bench, never considered a fast runner, used to steal a lot of bases that way.

You have to pick your times to run. The delayed steal is especially effective with a left-handed hitter at the plate, because the catcher will have trouble seeing the runner.

Another good stealing situation is with two outs, a below-average runner at first, and two strikes on an average hitter. The delayed steal can also be used at second base whenever the catcher drops to his knees before throwing back to the pitcher.

The delayed steal can make things happen by forcing the defense to make a mistake. If the runner can make second, a base hit will score him.

FLY BALLS

The golden rule for base runners is to freeze on all line drives and get back. After the runner sees the ball through the infield, he can advance to the next base safely.

Whenever there is a foul ball, the runner must tag up and read the play. This is the only way he can advance to the next base on a foul ball.

On certain fly balls that are hit deep in the outfield, the runner can tag up and advance to the next base. This is done only when the outfielder is under the ball ready to make a catch, and especially if the outfielder has a below-average arm.

If a ball is hit deep to the outfield and the outfielder must turn and sprint for the ball, the base runner needs to go as far off the base as possible.

The base runner should go as far as he can toward second base. In some cases, he will go all the way to second and may even round the base. If the outfielder makes the grab, the runner can return to first with no problem. In the event that the outfielder drops the ball, the runner can advance to third easily and may even score.

COACHING POINT

Anytime that you see the numbers on the outfielder's back, go as far as you can. If he is camped under the ball ready to make a catch, you can think about tagging up and advancing.

On pop-ups that are hit in the infield or shallow fly balls in the outfield, the runner wants to go as far as he can and still be able to get back to first. There is very little chance of advancing on a shallow pop-up. Some coaches tell their players to "go halfway." But halfway for some players is different than for others. So I say "go as far as you can."

Sometimes, on a deep fly ball, a runner can tag up and advance to second base. The runner must take into consideration the number of outs, the next hitter, and the importance of the run . . . however, he must not forget his own ability.

Mental Aspects for Players

Instruct your players to keep the following points in mind:

- Before you reach first base, do your homework. While in the dugout, study and know the pitcher's best move.
- Concentrate your thinking on stealing and getting a good jump. Try to remove all thoughts about getting picked off.
- Know if the pitcher has a quick pickoff move or a slow one.
- Be aware if the pitcher has a slow kick to the plate.
- Be sure to know if the catcher has a good release time (2.0 to 2.1 seconds).

DRILLS

Return to First Base Drill

PURPOSE: To teach players the proper mechanics in diving back into first base.

EQUIPMENT: Foul line in outfield, grassy area with throw-down bases

IMPLEMENTATION:

1. Have four players at a time line up about 10 feet away from the line.
2. Have a coach or player stand about 20 feet in front of them and come to the set position.
3. When the coach/player sets off and fakes a throw back to first, have the player dive back to first using proper form.
4. Also, as an alternative to the dive, have the player practice coming back to first standing up using proper form.

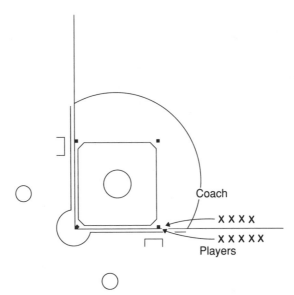

Figure 5.9

Straight Line Drill

PURPOSE: To teach players to take the cross-over step and remain in a straight line as they run toward second base.

EQUIPMENT: Grassy area, outfield foul lines, or a white chalk line drawn in the outfield grass

IMPLEMENTATION:

1. Have the players line up one at a time, starting with the left foot perpendicular to the straight line.
2. The right foot should be about toe to instep with a 45-degree angle.
3. On the coach's command, the player crosses over, with his left foot landing on the chalk line.
4. Each stride should land on the chalk line, giving the player maximum coverage on each step.

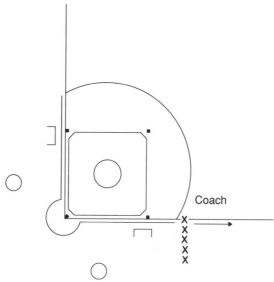

Coach

Figure 5.10

Cross-Over Drill

PURPOSE: To teach the batter the proper technique of crossing over and pivoting on the right foot.

EQUIPMENT: Grassy area in right field, outfield foul lines, batting gloves. (Can also be done inside.)

IMPLEMENTATION:

1. Have the players pair up, with one player in a stealing position and the other standing in front of him, just off his right foot.
2. The partner holds a batting glove in front of the runner, about waist high.
3. The stealer reaches with his left arm to grab the glove and then crosses over (see Figure 5.11).
4. As he grabs the glove, he crosses over with his left foot and pulls his left arm back in sync.
5. The grab and cross-over action puts the arms and legs in sync on the first step, helping the player develop the quickness needed to steal a base.

Figure 5.11a   **b**

c

CHAPTER 6

Going From Second to Third

The strategic aspect of baseball sharply intensifies as the runner reaches second base, especially with less than two out. The runner is now in scoring position, one base hit away from home plate, and the pressure level rises for both offense and defense.

The runner must remain aggressive and alert, ready to react intelligently to any contingency and any situation. His immediate purpose is to do everything he can to advance to third base—on a wild pitch, a pitch into the dirt, a tag-up on a fly ball, or even a steal.

The smart runner will try to steal the catcher's signs and relay them to the hitter. If, for example, he spots the fastball sign, he can pass it on to the hitter by the way he stands (a little more erect). See Figure 6.1a. If the sign is for a curveball, the runner can bend over a little more (Figure 6.1b).

Figure 6.1a   b

If the catcher signs inside or outside, the runner may relay the location by lifting an arm.

Even if the runner cannot read the signs, he should make the defense believe he has them. By inducing the defense to go to its second set of signals, he may create a little confusion, perhaps even a cross-up in the signs, and force a passed ball.

LEADS AT SECOND BASE

Before the runner steps off second, he should do four things:

1. Make sure he has the sign from the coach to know what's going on.
2. Check the number of outs.
3. Check the defense to see how it's playing the hitter.
4. Make sure the pitcher has the ball.

Primary Lead

Daring baseball starts with an aggressive lead at second base. I have runners walk off a five-step lead, like they do at first base (Figure 6.2). A comfortable primary lead is essential so that if the pitcher turns and throws, the runner can get back to second with a step and a dive. Good communication is imperative. You never want to see your runners trying to get a big lead while the coach is yelling "Back!" and the ball is going to the plate. I want the runner to get a 12- to 15-foot lead and then hold it until he moves

Figure 6.2a   **b**

c

into his secondary lead. With less than two outs, I want the runner to move in a straight line toward third base. With two outs, I want him to move back a couple of steps behind an imaginary straight line from second to third base (Figure 6.3).

Figure 6.3

Secondary Lead

An aggressive secondary lead can produce a lot of extra runs during the season. The runner should take two hard shuffle steps that put him out about 18 to 20 feet from the base (Figure 6.4). I want him to land on his right foot as the ball is entering the hitting zone, and to read the ball off the bat.

If the ball is hit directly at or behind him, he'll be able to advance to third base. If, however, the ball is hit in front of him, he should wait for it to go through the infield. Exception to this rule: a chopper to the third baseman that forces him to charge about 15 feet in and throw to first base.

COACHING POINT

The runner must never cross his feet as the catcher is receiving the ball. If he does, the catcher will be able to throw down to second and pick him off.

As the catcher receives the ball, the runner should push off with his right foot and cross over a step or two back to second. This will prevent the catcher from picking him off.

Figure 6.4a

b

c

d

THE SACRIFICE BUNT

If the manager decides to bunt, the runner must concentrate his efforts on getting to third base. If he doesn't do his job at second base, the defense will have a chance of getting him at third even on a perfect bunt.

Before advancing with a secondary lead, the runner has to make sure that the pitcher throws the ball to home. Again, I want the runner to take a secondary lead with two shuffle steps, landing on his right foot. It's imperative that the runner not cross over until he sees that the ball is bunted on the ground.

COACHING POINT

A common fault with aggressive base runners is that they'll cross over to get a good jump and wind up in no-man's land on a missed bunt. The catcher will come up and nail him at second or get him in a rundown. Instruct your players never to cross over until they see the ball on the ground.

The runner has to watch the pitcher for an inside move— that is, kicking up and continuing right into a pickoff move to second base. The runner must take his primary lead before sliding up, making sure the pitcher kicks and throws to the plate.

The runner cannot allow the pitcher to turn and pick him off. Because the shortstop will be holding him as close to the bag as possible, making him jitter around, the runner must read the pitcher before sliding up into an aggressive secondary lead. In short, he must read the ball from the mound to the plate, then read the ball off the bat.

If the ball is bunted on the ground, he must break toward third, reading the play as he runs. If the hitter misses the ball or takes the pitch, the runner must be balanced enough to reverse quickly back to second.

THE BUNT AND STEAL

The fake of a bunt can often be as effective as the bunt itself. A good fake bunt can allow the runner to steal third while the third baseman is moving in for a play.

You can also go for the run with a variation of this play. As the runner (at second) dashes for third, the hitter drag bunts or push bunts down the third-base line. Because the third baseman will almost always throw to first, the runner hits third and keeps on going to the plate.

The play will often catch the defense sleeping and give your team an easy run.

COACHING POINT

The runner at second must have average to above-average speed. A slow runner will have a difficult time going all the way to the plate. But even an average runner can make this play work, because the first baseman will often be caught napping on the throw to first. Or the surprise advance can make him throw wildly to the plate.

TAGGING UP ON FLY BALLS

Golden rule number 1 on tagging up on fly balls is this: With no outs, tag up; with one out, go halfway. The reasoning is simple: With no outs, the runner wants to reach third base. I don't like to abide by this rule. I prefer to tell my players, "Go as far as you can go and still get back," regardless of where the ball is hit.

Remember, golden rule number 2 is never to make the first or third out at third base. You don't want to run yourself out of an inning. The runner must use common sense and check the ball closely. If it is a shallow fly ball, there's no way he's going to be able to advance to third. So he should go as far as he can go and still be able to get back to second if the play is made.

A deep fly ball also calls for a common-sense approach—that is, the runner should tag up and go to third, especially if you're playing in a deep ballpark.

Whenever an outfielder is running after a fly ball and you can see the numbers on his back, you want the runner to hang out and go as far off the base as he possibly can. Your players have to understand that once the fielder camps under the ball, deep up against the warning track or fence, the runner will not be able to come back, tag up, and go to third base.

If a runner has just average to below-average speed, he must again use common sense. He'll never be able to tag up and advance to the next base. He must, therefore, "hang out" as far as he can; and if the fielder makes the catch, he must go back to second. If the fielder happens to drop the ball, the runner might be able to score on the play. If the runner can see that the fielder is going to camp under the deep fly ball, he must immediately go back to the bag, tag up, and be prepared to go to third.

Proper technique for tagging up: If the ball is hit to left center or left field, the runner puts the right foot on the bag in sprinter fashion and looks over his right shoulder toward center and left field.

If the ball is hit into right center or right field, the runner puts the left foot on the base in a sprinter stance and looks over his left shoulder, ready to advance to third.

As the runner goes to third, he must concentrate on the third-base coach's signal. It will tell him whether to stand up or slide, and what side (left or right) to slide on.

Whenever a foul ball is hit down the left-field or the right-field line, remember that the only way the runner can advance is by tagging up. Instruct your players to be alert for the circus catch, where a fielder comes running across the foul line into foul territory, makes a dramatic catch, and rolls over a couple of times. This will usually give the runner a good opportunity to sneak over to third base.

The runner must also be on the alert for a fielder who makes a great catch and forgets about the runner at second. Again, he may be able to sneak over to third base.

STEALING THIRD BASE

A good runner on third puts a lot of additional pressure on the pitcher, and also forces the middle infielders out of position, allowing a routine ground ball to sneak through.

Isn't it difficult to steal third, with the bag only 90 feet from the plate? Not really. You have to remember that you can get a much bigger lead at second because of the positioning of the shortstop and second baseman.

The runner at second is often able to get a walking lead, which will allow him to cover more ground and get an outstanding jump on the pitcher.

One of the best times to steal third is with one out. An aggressive team will try it with no outs or two outs just to establish its running game. Again, remember that golden rule: Never make the first or third out at third base, because you're in scoring position at second.

If you're going to steal with two outs or no outs, make sure you steal on the pitcher and that there is no chance of a close throw whatsoever. Some coaches—like me—will allow the runner to steal with two outs, especially if the hitter has been struggling that day. The catcher may overthrow third and allow the runner to score, whereas if you let the batter hit, he'd have to produce a solid hit to get the man in from second base. The steal becomes the percentage play in this situation.

When he's stealing third, I want the runner to get a little bigger primary lead than usual—a six-step rather than a five-step lead. The extra step is essential, and I also want the runner to be in a straight line between second and third.

If, with two outs, the runner is in a belly-back lead, or a couple of steps behind the straight line, it's very important to move him in on a straight line between second and third.

We expect our base runners or coaches, or both, to have done their job in the dugout—to have noticed what type of pitcher is on the mound. If he's a one-looker or a two-looker, we want to know whether he looks at the runner at second, turns, picks up his mitt, and then kicks and goes to the plate. If he does this, we know we can steal on him all day (Figure 6.5).

Some other questions need to be answered:

- Is the pitcher slow to the plate?
- Does he have a high kick or a low kick?
- Does he like to throw to second base?
- Do the shortstop and second baseman do a great job of holding runners? Or do they go to sleep?

The defense will often allow the runner to get a bigger lead with two outs, putting the infielders back where a ball cannot sneak through them. Such defenses are inviting your runner to steal third, where he can score on a passed ball or wild pitch.

Another important consideration is stealing the catcher's signs. If the runner knows when a breaking ball is coming,

Figure 6.5a

b

c

d

and the pitcher is semi-slow to the plate, the runner has a good chance to steal third, because the ball will take longer getting to the plate.

Suppose your number-four hitter is at the plate. Has the pitcher been starting your power hitters off with a breaking ball? If so, the runner may think of going on the first pitch.

You also want your third-base coach to help your runners steal third. If the runner has a good aggressive lead, and the second baseman and shortstop come in to kick him around, I have our third-base coach yell, "Hold it! Hold it! Hold it!" as the infielders start returning to their positions. This tells the runner that the shortstop and second baseman are no longer holding him on, and he can now be more aggressive.

If the second baseman or shortstop does make a pickoff attempt, the third-base coach must yell, "Back! Back! Back! Back! Back!"

If the infielder moves directly behind the runner or close by him, the coach must yell, "Right there! Right there! Right there!"

These calls allow the runner to know exactly what the second baseman or shortstop is doing without having to turn back to see.

You'll often see a runner look back after the pitcher has already turned to throw. That's how a lot of runners get picked off at second. The third-base coach is actually the eyes of the runner at second.

The runner takes the primary lead aggressively but intelligently. Having done his homework in the dugout, he is now ready to steal third. Let's say the pitcher is a one-looker. He comes set, checks the runner, turns his head, then kicks and goes to the plate.

When the pitcher checks him, the runner has his good primary lead. Then, as the pitcher turns his head, the runner takes an additional slide up. Remember, you want the runner to slide up as the pitcher turns his head, which prevents him from seeing any movement as he turns to pick up the plate.

COACHING POINT

A lot of pitchers will turn their heads, pick up the plate, and then kick and deliver. This gives the runner a second and a half to slide off the base and a couple of seconds to get an additional lead. This is, in effect, an additional slide-up or an additional primary lead.

Summing up: The runner has his primary lead; then, when the pitcher turns his head, the runner gets that additional secondary lead, putting him about 18 to 20 feet off the base—in great position to steal third.

Unless the runner has tremendous speed, or unless the pitcher is extremely slow to the plate, the runner will find it almost impossible to steal from a primary lead. He must get an additional secondary lead—the kind of walking lead that will give him the momentum he needs for the takeoff. That's how the average runner can get to steal third.

Even if the pitcher throws a curveball, it will be very difficult for the defense to make the play and get the runner out at third base. Many times with an average runner, you will tell him curveball, and if he gets the curveball, then he can come on. Then you will have a sign to let him know that a breaking ball is coming and to run! If he gets a good jump, and if the pitcher throws a curveball, even the average to below-average runner has a chance to steal third base.

Let's face it. If the pitcher throws the curveball and it goes into the dirt, the catcher will have to pull the ball out of the dirt, come up with a great throw, and put it right on the money; and the third baseman will have to catch it and make the proper tag to have any chance of getting the runner at third. There are a lot of maybes in there for the defense, and the percentage is with the runner.

It is imperative for the hitter to take the curveball when he sees the runner getting a good jump with fewer than two strikes. Once the runner gets to third, he can advance on a fly ball, a ground ball, a drag bunt, a wild pitch, or a passed ball. So it's essential that the hitter take a breaking ball or off-speed pitch that will allow the runner to slide safely into third.

Anytime the runner gets a great jump, I expect the hitter to take the pitch—even a fastball—with fewer than two strikes. A lot of smart pitchers will check a runner once or twice, and, as he turns his head, kick and throw to the plate. This makes it very difficult to steal third. The runner must now get into the pitcher's timing or rhythm. Many pitchers go through a ritual: check the runner, kick, and turn at the same time. But there's a split second in there (one-thousand-one, one-thousand-two) before he goes to the plate.

I tell our runners to count, "One-thousand-one, one-thousand-" and jump on "two." If the pitcher kicks and goes to the plate at the same time, the runner can get an additional slide up, and then be off and running. In short, we look for some type of timing device to steal third.

ADVANCING TO THIRD BASE ON GROUND BALLS

As I stated earlier, in taking a lead off second, the runner must remind himself to hold up on a ball hit in front of him, and to freeze and get back on all line drives.

There are exceptions, of course. One would be a slow roller to the third baseman that forces him to come in, pick up the ball, and throw to first.

Another exception might be a chopper between third and short that forces the third baseman to take a drop step back almost into the outfield grass or that brings the short-stop over, enabling the runner to advance to third.

Another would be if the third baseman has to move left into the infield grass to field a slow chopper, allowing the runner to advance as the infielder makes the play.

Or the third baseman will sometimes field the ball, never looking at the runner (at second), and make the play to first. If the third baseman fails to freeze the runner, he can extend his lead and, as soon as the fielder releases the ball, break for third. The runner should try to advance to third on any ball hit directly at him or to his left. On a ball hit directly at him, by the time he takes his secondary lead and turns and goes, the shortstop will make that play on his forehand side. When the shortstop has to go to his left for the ball, he will be forced to stop, plant, wheel, and throw to third, making it very difficult to get the runner going into third.

If the ball is bunted or tapped in front of the plate, the runner must watch what the catcher does when he comes up with the ball. If the catcher looks to second and freezes the runner, the runner must stay at second. If the catcher forgets about the runner or immediately goes to first with the ball, the runner has a good chance to advance to third.

Mental Aspects for Players

Instruct your players to keep the following points in mind when at second base:

- Look to see if you can steal the signs from the catcher.
- Give a signal to the hitter telling him where the catcher is setting up—on the inside or outside part of the plate.
- Make sure that a ground ball is behind you before you try to advance to third.
- With two outs, remember to belly back behind second base for a proper angle. This is approximately three steps back behind the imaginary straight line between second and third.
- Look to see if the pitcher is giving away his pitches by showing his grip in the glove.
- Be aggressive in your secondary lead so you can score on a base hit.

DRILLS

Baserunning Drill I

PURPOSE: To teach the runner when and how to advance to third base.

EQUIPMENT: Baseball and fungo bat

IMPLEMENTATION:

1. Have the runners set up at second base and go two at a time as a coach fungos the ball between third and short, directly at the runner (at second), or to his left.
2. Next, have each player work on reading the ball off the fungo, checking to see whether it is in front of him or behind him.

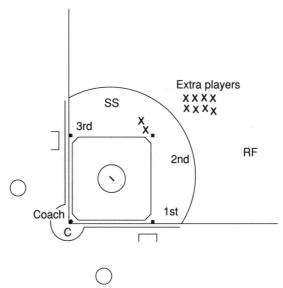

Figure 6.6

Baserunning Drill II

PURPOSE: To teach the runners how to steal third base.

EQUIPMENT: Balls, infield

IMPLEMENTATION:

1. Put a coach on the mound and set up three runners at second base.
2. Have the coach come to a set position and go through a certain routine—one-looker or two-looker, and so on.
3. Have the runner read the pitcher, try to slide up with a secondary lead, and steal third.
4. Have the coach change his rhythm or his looks to give the runner variety in reading the pitcher.

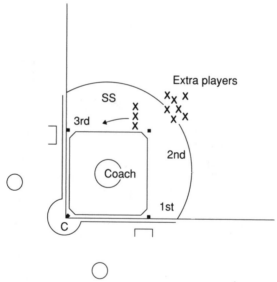

Figure 6.7

Baserunning Drill III

PURPOSE: To teach the runners how to tag up at second.

EQUIPMENT: Fungo bat, balls, full field

IMPLEMENTATION:

1. Place several runners at second base, a coach at home plate (with a fungo bat), and a player in each outfield position (left, center, and right).
2. Have the coach hit fungos—line drives and pop-ups to the outfield—and let the runners react accordingly, reading the play and either holding or, if possible, advancing to the next base.

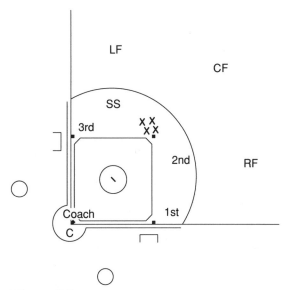

Figure 6.8

CHAPTER 7

Advancing From Third to Home

Once the base runner reaches third base, he must concentrate on three responsibilities:

1. Tagging up on all fly balls and line drives
2. Scoring on the ordinary, routine ground ball
3. Putting pressure on the defense, while continuing to study the coach for signs, checking the defense, and keeping track of the number of outs and every other relevant factor in the situation

COACHING POINT

The golden rule to remember on any ball hit into the air is this: "Tag up" or "Get back." And remember: The runner must freeze on all line drives and get back!

With no outs, the runner at third must wait for the ball to go through before coming in, unless he feels that he can score easily, such as on a high chopper over the mound. With one out, he must read the play, but be thinking *home*.

A good aggressive team will not waste the opportunity to score. They will literally try to steal home. This is why I like a walking lead at third base. It allows the runner to score on close plays even with the infield in.

I have our players work on their leads (especially at third) after they have taken pregame batting practice.

WALKING LEAD

The base runner (at third) takes his primary lead in foul territory, with his eyes on the pitcher (Figure 7.1). He never takes his eyes off the pitcher. That is why he gets his sign from the coach while standing on the base.

He then moves about 3 feet into foul territory, where he cannot be called out in the event that he is hit by a batted ball.

Starting with his left foot on the base, he takes five normal steps toward home, ending on his right foot. This is his primary lead. From this point, he moves into his secondary lead by taking a step with his left foot and then another step with his right foot (Figure 7.2).

He tries to time it so he will land on his right foot as the ball is about to enter the hitting zone, allowing him to get an excellent jump on a ground ball or passed ball.

The runner must remember to follow the ball from the mound to the plate. This will keep him from being picked off third by a pitcher, as well as enable him to instantly advance on balls in the dirt.

Figure 7.1a
b

c
d

e

Figure 7.2a

b

c

RETURNING TO THE BASE

As the runner lands on his right foot (just before the ball enters the hitting zone), one of two things is likely to happen: The catcher will catch the ball, or the hitter will hit the ball.

If the ball is hit, the runner must read the play and react. If the catcher catches the ball, the runner must return to third base.

The runner must always be on the alert for a pickoff attempt. The moment the catcher indicates pickoff, the runner should push off his right foot and cross over toward third base *in fair territory*—making it very difficult for the catcher to get a good view of the third baseman. The catcher will either have to throw around the runner (creating a chance for a bad throw) or hit the runner in the back. The odds are all in the runner's favor. As the runner starts back to the bag, he can check the third baseman to see if he is breaking for the base. Sometimes, the catcher will bluff a throw. The runner shouldn't dive back unless a pickoff attempt is in progress.

GROUND-BALL SITUATIONS

I have basically three verbal signs for my runner at third:

1. "Make the ball go through."
2. "Must go."
3. "On your own—read it."

"Make the ball go through" is self-explanatory. If the ball gets through the infield, the runner will have no trouble scoring. This verbal sign is usually given with no outs or the infield in. Other situations that can dictate this call are the score or late innings.

"Must go" means break for the plate on any ground ball. If the ball gets through, is hit slowly, or is mishandled, the runner will have a chance to score. This is why it's essential for the runner to read the ball off the bat and get a good jump.

I often use this verbal sign with runners at first and third and one out (or no outs). If the runner is thrown out at home, we will still have first and second and two outs (or one out). What we're trying to do is stay out of a double play that can kill our inning. I'd rather have first and second with one out than a man on third and two outs. We always keep in mind who's on deck. He might be the man to win the ball game for us. So we try to give him a chance!

On a "must go" sign, I also want my players to read the play. For example, if a ball is hit to the third baseman and our runner at third is dead out, I want him to stop and get into a rundown—to stay alive as long as possible, allowing the hitter to advance to second and any other runners to move up a base.

COACHING POINT

As you know, many things can go wrong in a rundown. The defense can drop the ball, miss a tag, or even throw the ball away. Or you might even be lucky enough to get an obstruction call. Take anything that the "pressure play" gives you.

"Read it on your own" is a very tough sign for the runner. It permits him to read the defense and the play and decide whether he can score. He must take into consideration his own speed and athletic ability, coupled with the defensive alignment, the speed of ground balls, and their location.

If the runner misjudges the play, he must get into a rundown unless it is a close play.

With the defense back at normal depth, he usually should be able to score, especially when the ball is hit to the shortstop, second baseman, or first baseman.

Balls hit directly to the third baseman are tough to score on, whereas balls hit to the third baseman's left make it very difficult for him to plant, change direction, and get off an accurate throw.

The ball hit directly back to the pitcher is almost impossible to score on. The runner should make sure the ball goes through or bounces over the pitcher's head before attempting to score.

TAGGING UP ON FLY BALLS

As previously mentioned, the golden rule is to tag up on all fly balls. The coach's only responsibility is to remind the runner to tag up and then tell him whether he wants him to try to score.

Figure 7.3 shows the proper way to tag up. If the ball is hit anywhere from left field toward the right-field foul line, the runner (on third) should place his left foot on the bag and turn his body toward the catcher, putting him in excellent running position.

Figure 7.3

The runner should then glance over his left shoulder and read the ball entering the outfielder's glove.

COACHING POINT

I'd rather have the runner read the play than have the coach read it and tell the runner when to go. It's faster for the runner to direct read than to wait to react on a command.

If the ball is hit down the left-field line in foul territory, I want the runner to tag with his right foot and glance over his right shoulder (Figure 7.4).

Figure 7.4

Regardless of the type of fly ball—line drive, pop-up, sinking line, deep fly ball, foul ball—the runner must tag up. If the ball is mishandled, the runner will still have an excellent chance of scoring.

COACHING POINT

Make sure runners always tag up on foul fly balls. They might get a chance to advance.

The only exception to the rule about tagging up on fly balls is the pop-up in the infield or just behind it. If the ball is caught, the runner will not be able to advance. But if he moves off the base and the ball is dropped or bobbled, he might be able to sneak home.

If, with runners on first and third, the ball is hit into foul territory, both runners should tag up and start for the next base.

If the throw goes to second, the lead runner can score and the back runner can stop and get back to first. If the throw goes home, the back runner can advance to second and the lead runner can stop and go back to third base. The key is to have the runners break and read the throw.

Whenever a runner is attempting to score from third, a well-coached on-deck hitter will position himself 10 to 12 feet behind the plate and give a hand sign to the runner.

Two hands up will mean stand up, two hands down will mean slide.

SQUEEZE PLAYS

I like to use three types of squeeze plays: the safety, the fake squeeze, and the suicide.

The Safety Squeeze

This play allows the runner to break for home *after* he sees the bunt on the ground. He must read the ball as it approaches the strike zone, and must look for the best possible jump. At the same time, he wants to extend his secondary lead a little more than usual. In the event of a missed bunt, he must hurry back to third.

The hitter should show bunt as the pitcher's arm starts down just before the release. The hitter must bunt only at a strike, nudging the ball by the pitcher and toward the second baseman, making it very difficult for the second baseman or first baseman to defense the play. The element of surprise is a big factor in the success of the play.

The Fake Squeeze

You can use this play to put additional pressure on the defense—to play mind games with the defenders. A great time for this play is with the bases loaded, a 3-1 count, and an average to below-average hitter at the plate.

If the pitcher chokes and hesitates the least bit in his delivery, he just might throw ball four and present you with a run. Remember, all pitchers are taught to pitch out on a squeeze, and you hope to take advantage of the player who isn't thinking. The slightest hesitation can mean ball four.

Another good situation for the fake squeeze is with runners on first and third and one out. Have the back runner light out for second base as the pitcher kicks and throws to the plate.

The hitter shows bunt, and the runner at third takes one hard step and yells "Squeeze!" More times than not, the defense will think squeeze . . . and the back runner will slide into second without a play!

The runner at third should be careful not to move too much off third when he fakes the squeeze. He should shorten his primary lead so that he can get back to third with no problem.

The Suicide Squeeze

This is a kamikaze play. Once you start, there's no turning back. The runner must break from third as the pitcher's arm starts forward to keep the pitcher from adjusting his throw. It is vital for the hitter to be prepared to bunt the ball no matter where it is pitched. If he's ready for a bad pitch, he will not be surprised when one is thrown. He *must* get a piece of the ball, or the runner is dead.

Both runner and hitter must be careful not to alert the defense too soon. An alert pitcher will be able to pitch out and put the offense in deep trouble.

The hitter must also make sure not to be too fine with his bunt. All he has to do is get the ball down in fair territory, and the runner will score. Overly meticulous bunters bunt a lot of foul balls.

STEALING HOME

Believe it or not, many hours are spent on this at UT. The goal is to steal home 5 to 10 times in a 75-game schedule. I consider a 70 percent success ratio pretty good.

Normally, we try to steal with less than two outs and fewer than two strikes on the hitter. It doesn't matter if the pitcher is left-handed or right-handed.

The two keys we look for when stealing home are (1) Can the pitcher freeze the runner? and (2) How slow is the pitcher to the plate?

If the pitcher doesn't check the runner before starting his windup, the runner has an excellent chance of stealing

Figure 7.5a

b

c

home. If the pitcher is also slow to the plate, so much the better (Figure 7.5).

Some pitchers will check the runner but then take 3.5 seconds to deliver to the plate. When turning the head back to home to pick up the catcher, the pitcher will automatically begin his windup. I have our runner break for home as soon as the pitcher turns his head (Figure 7.6).

The pitcher must force the runner to take just a moderate lead off third. If he cannot freeze the runner, the latter can extend his lead to 15 to 18 feet.

The smart coach will time the pitcher from the moment he moves until the ball is caught by the catcher. A good time is around 3.2 seconds. When you find a pitcher around 3.5 from windup to plate, you have a man you can steal home on.

In practice, I like to time my players from their stealing lead to the slide into home. This gives me some indication as to their ability to steal home. If my runner averages 3.0 seconds and the pitcher is 3.2, I know my man has a chance.

I want the runner to cautiously extend his lead as far as possible without drawing attention to himself. As soon as the pitcher begins his windup, the runner breaks for the plate and executes a pop-up slide to the front corner.

COACHING POINT

The headfirst slide is dangerous at home plate.

The hitter must show bunt to keep the catcher back in his position. At the last moment, we want the hitter to pull the bat back and give room to the sliding runner. If executed properly, stealing home is a good risk (Figure 7.7).

Fake Steal

A lot of young pitchers will lose their concentration and balk when they see a runner breaking for the plate. You can get the same effect with a fake steal. You can have the runner wait until the pitcher checks him before throwing

Figure 7.6a

b

c

Figure 7.7a

b

c

d

home. At this precise moment, the runner can take one hard cross-over step toward home and induce the pitcher to flinch his hands or step off improperly or balk. Result: an easy run.

A pitcher who loses concentration may also wild pitch or just throw ball four. All of this again gives the edge to an aggressive team.

As I said earlier, at third our team is always ready to try to steal a run.

First and Third Stealing Home

This play is often used, especially in high school ball, with two outs and a below-average hitter at the plate.

The runner at first breaks for second and looks back in to read the throw to the plate. If the catcher comes up throwing to second, the runner from first pulls up halfway down the baseline. Then, as the defense proceeds with a rundown, the runner on third breaks for the plate.

The back runner tries to stay alive long enough for the front runner to score. If your team must make an out, it has to be at home. It is imperative that you force the defense to throw to the plate. The defense will often throw the ball away, be late with the throw, or try to tag the runner at first, allowing the run to score.

Some teams will allow the back runner to steal and either throw back to the pitcher to entice the front runner to break for home, or throw to third.

In either case, you have runners at second and third with two outs. A base hit will score two runs.

Mental Aspects for Players

Your players should keep the following points in mind when they're at third base:

- Always check to see if the pitcher looks back at you before he starts his windup.

- Make sure you take your lead in foul territory.
- Check the defense to see if they are playing back or in.
- Look to see if the pitcher is giving away his pitches in his glove.
- Remind yourself to tag up on all fly balls.

DRILLS

Tag-Up Drill

PURPOSE: To teach players the proper technique of tagging up at third base.

EQUIPMENT: Set up on third-base side of diamond or with several throw-down bases in the outfield

IMPLEMENTATION:

1. Have the players line up at third base, one at a time.
2. Position a player or coach in the outfield grass, simulating catching a ball.
3. Have the player at third take a lead and then, on command, break back to the base, using the proper technique.
4. Have the player read the catch and then break for the plate.

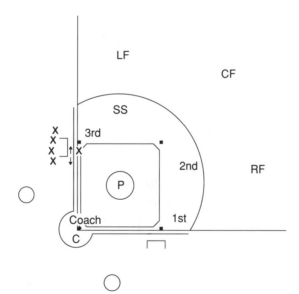

Figure 7.8

Stealing Home Drill

PURPOSE: To teach players the proper technique of stealing home. This drill allows the runner to really
see how it works.

EQUIPMENT: Infield area, using the mound, home plate,
and third-base areas; can also be done in the
outfield or in the gym using throw-down
bases

IMPLEMENTATION:

1. Have the player take his stealing lead while focusing
   in on the pitcher.
2. Have four players go at a time (see Figure 7.9) to help
   speed up the drill and get more players involved.
3. Have the pitcher go through a windup throw to a
   catcher.
4. Do this several times, and then do it live with a hitter
   and catcher.

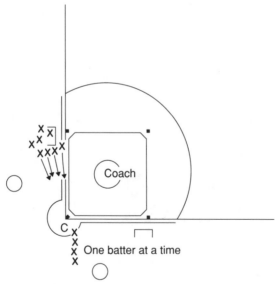

Figure 7.9

CHAPTER 8

Sliding

An aggressive baserunning team must pay a lot of attention to sliding. It is the icing on the base runner's cake. A runner who cannot slide is like a pitcher with a great fastball but no breaking ball to go with it.

In teaching players to slide, I take them into the outfield and have them sit down cross-legged. The leg a player instinctively tucks under will probably be his sliding leg. I try to determine the side that feels natural and comfortable to each player. I encourage the players who are comfortable on either side to practice on both sides. Such versatility will give them an advantage. But, though I'd like everyone to be able to slide on both sides, it isn't really a must.

Once the players have determined their more comfortable side, I have them pair up. One partner (the ''slider'') sits on the ground and puts one leg under and the other straight out. His partner then pulls him around, first while the slider is sitting on the side of his thigh, and then while the slider is resting squarely on his buttocks.

I want to know which side *he* finds easier, though I know it's easier and safer to slide on the buttocks.

In the beginning, we use a grassy area in the outfield that has been wetted down beforehand. Then the players remove their spikes and slide in their socks. This takes the fear out of sliding and lets the players have fun while they learn the skill.

COACHING POINT

Do not soak the area too much, or the players will lose body control while sliding.

There are basically four reasons to slide:

1. To avoid a tag
2. To break momentum
3. To break up a double play
4. To avoid a collision

The first step in the actual teaching process is teaching players how to fall. That's what sliding is—*controlled falling*. It is important for players not to tense up or be hesitant about sliding. Indecisiveness is fatal. The runner has to relax, and he must *never* change his mind once he decides to hit the dirt. Otherwise, he can catch a spike and sustain an injury. Once he learns the correct technique, he will gain confidence and find it easier to relax.

I like to teach players several ways to slide, most of which stem from the oldest and best slide in the book—the bent-leg slide. The bent-leg is simple, safe, quick, and versatile. You cannot ask more of a slide.

THE BENT-LEG SLIDE

As the runner approaches the base, he must make up his mind to slide and then go into it without hesitation ("He who hesitates gets injured"). The runner should start his slide about 10 feet from the base. He should "sit down," never leap into the slide, and let his momentum take him into the base.

The extended leg should be slightly flexed so the slider avoids jamming his knee, with the toes pointed straight up and about 6 inches off the ground (Figure 8.1).

The upper body should be in a sit-up position with the shoulders squared to the base, allowing the runner to keep his body squarely over his buttocks.

The hands should be kept up close to the chest and relaxed, not on the ground.

Figure 8.1a

b

c

d

COACHING POINT

The players should not try to break the fall with their hands or trail them behind on the ground. That's a surefire way of abrading the hands and wrists.

A lot of players will wear a batting glove or pick up a handful of dirt to protect the hands from injury.

The bent-leg slide is a very versatile slide. Once the players master it, I encourage them to learn the different ways of utilizing it.

POP-UP SLIDE WITH BENT LEG

This employs the same fundamentals as the bent-leg, except that the runner pops up into position to immediately advance on a bad throw or any throw that gets away from the fielder.

The runner must start the pop-up slide closer to the base (about 8 feet instead of 10). As he approaches the base with his leg extended, he must remember to stay in a sit-up position, not lean back or to the side, because this will make it almost impossible to pop up.

As before, the extended leg is slightly bent and about 5 to 6 inches off the ground.

The runner should come into the base with the instep of the extended foot. As the contact is made, he should lean forward and thrust the center of gravity forward, letting his momentum pop him right up so that he can continue to the next base, if feasible (Figure 8.2).

If the runner can slide on either leg, he'd do well to slide with his left leg tucked under. This will allow him to pop up and continue right on to third with his left foot.

If he slides with his right leg tucked under, he would have to take a jab step with his right foot (toward right field) to gain balance and then a jab step toward third with his left foot. That extra step could mean the difference between being out or being safe on a close play at third. Remember, the key to the success of the bent-leg slide is for

Figure 8.2a   **b**

c   d

the player to remain squarely over the buttocks with the shoulders square to the base.

HOOK SLIDE WITH BENT LEG

A runner uses the hook slide to avoid a tag when the ball has beaten the runner but is somewhat off-target. For example, if the catcher throws to the second baseman's right on a steal attempt, the runner will want to slide into the right-field corner of the base. This will make it extremely difficult for the second baseman to reach for the baseball and then come all the way back to the base for the tag.

The slider must lean his upper body back to avoid being tagged on the shoulder and, as he nears the base, he should reach in and grab the corner of the base with his hand. He must be sure to focus in on the corner of the base and hold on.

The key to the bent-leg slide is for the runner to get an arm's length (2 feet) away from the base and start the slide about 8 to 10 feet from the base (Figure 8.3).

Notice in the photos how the runner concentrates on grabbing the corner of the base. If he were sliding to the infield side, he would grab the inside corner of the bag with his right hand.

Notice that this isn't what you would normally call a *hook* slide. The foot isn't really hooked. I prefer this approach for four reasons:

- Advantage 1: I believe it is a quicker and easier way of avoiding an off-the-line throw.
- Advantage 2: It also eliminates the possibility of the foot coming off the bag (a danger in the hook slide) and protects the slider from picking up strawberries.
- Advantage 3: The bent-leg hook slide puts the runner in better position to pop up and advance on an overthrow.
- Advantage 4: A runner trying to stretch a single into a double on a throw coming from right field can, on a close play, avoid the tag with a bent-leg hook to the infield side of the bag.

FLIP-FLOP (OR BACK-DOOR) SLIDE WITH BENT LEG

The flip-flop slide is used when the ball beats the runner to the bag and the baseman is waiting to tag him out. The

Figure 8.3a   b

c   d

e

runner's objective is to get the baseman to reach out and tag the runner instead of dropping his glove in front of the base and letting the runner tag himself out.

COACHING POINT

It would be foolish for the runner to slide directly into the tag. He should make the defense work for the out. The best chance he has is to get to the bag via the back door.

The runner must again start with the bent-leg slide, starting it about 8 to 10 feet from the base and an arm's distance out (2 feet).

As he approaches the bag—say, second—he should reach in with his left hand to decoy the baseman. As the baseman tries to tag the hand, the runner should pull it away and go by the base. At the right moment, he should flip-flop and reach back to tag the rear of the bag with his right hand (Figure 8.4).

Second basemen are usually taught to take the throw at the base and let the runner tag himself out by sliding into the glove. The back-door route can catch them unprepared.

BENT-LEG SLIDE AT HOME AND AT FIRST

Because these are the only bases with which the runner does not have to maintain contact, all he has to do is touch them before being tagged. That's why you often find the catcher setting up in front of home plate, leaving the back unguarded. He will try to intimidate the runner first, then reach out to get the throw and step back to get the runner.

The first thing the runner going into home plate wants to do is avoid a collision (if possible). He doesn't want to go into anyone who's wearing all that heavy protective equipment.

The key for the runner is to get up enough momentum to carry him *past* the plate. He must start sliding when he's about 8 feet away and at least an arm's distance out from the plate.

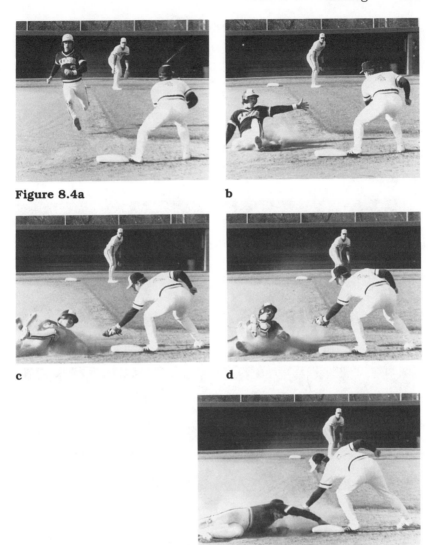

Figure 8.4a   b

c   d

e

As he slides by the plate, the runner can reach in and make a tag with his left hand, then pull his hand back quickly. This will not leave a lot for the catcher to tag or much time to do it, particularly on a close play (Figure 8.5).

The same pop-tag slide can be used at first base whenever an infield throw pulls the first baseman off the bag toward the inside. The runner can avoid the lunging baseman by

Figure 8.5a   b

c   d

e   f

sliding by the bag and making a quick tag with his left hand as he slides by.

BREAKING UP THE DOUBLE PLAY VIA THE BENT-LEG

Breaking up a double play can be very dangerous for both the runner and the pivot man. We know that a lot of runners are taught to wipe out the pivot man "any way you can" . . . and that includes illegally sliding out of the base-line to get into his legs or hitting him with a roll block.

I think that's a bush play that should never be encouraged by a coach.

The purpose of the bent-leg slide in this situation is to keep the pivot man from getting off his throw or to force him to make a bad throw (Figure 8.6).

Figure 8.6a   b

c

The runner must first read the pivot man's route—inside or outside. He must then start his bent-leg slide about 8 feet from the base. After impacting the ground, he should lean slightly toward the bent-leg side but not hold his hands up to interfere with the throw. He should hold his hands in front of his face to protect against a foot or a knee.

The runner must stay up a little so as to force the pivot man into the air. This could cause him to hold onto the ball or get off a poor throw.

Remember, the runner must stay within reach of the bag or risk an interference call by the umpire. The high school and college rule states that the runner must slide directly into the base without popping up. If he does pop up, the umpire can allow the double play.

HEADFIRST SLIDE

This is a quick, exciting, aggressive slide, especially when a Pete Rose is doing it. Probably because of Rose, more and more sliders are now doing it. Witness Rickey Henderson and Vince Coleman, perhaps the cream of the current crop of base-stealers.

In Figure 8.7, notice how the player glides on top of the ground. He doesn't jump into the base. As he approaches the bag, he extends his arms and bends his elbows slightly to avoid jamming a shoulder. He contacts the ground simultaneously with his hands, arms, chest, and legs, keeping his head up to see the bag and to track the throw.

As previously mentioned, it's a good idea to keep the fingers up to avoid jamming them. Also note that the runner can use his arms to push himself up quickly into running position on a bad throw.

Once the runners have mastered the headfirst slide, they can start using it to go inside or outside the base. The runner will now slide to the outfield side or infield side to touch the corner of the base with his left hand or right hand.

The runner who gets a bad jump on a steal attempt will have to slide to the outfield side to avoid a tag.

COACHING POINT

The closer the play, the farther the runner will have to slide from the base and reach in (with his right hand in this case).

Figure 8.7a

b

c

Headfirst is also the quickest way to get back to first on a pickoff attempt.

COACHING POINT

A would-be stealer who doesn't have to dive back to first on a pickoff attempt is probably not taking enough of a lead.

Figure 8.8 shows the runner pivoting on his left foot and diving back to the bag. Observe how his hand hits the ground about 12 inches away and goes into the bag, keeping the slider from jamming a shoulder. Also notice the fingers pointing up and how the slider keeps his head up to check for bad throws that will enable him to advance.

Figure 8.9 shows the same play from a different angle. The runner takes his lead off the back corner of the base, enabling him to dive to the back corner or outfield side of the base and touch it with his right hand, giving the first baseman a more difficult tag to make.

The criticism of the headfirst slide is that it is "dangerous" and "not as quick." Untrue. Study the slide more closely and you will see that it is quicker and safer than the conventional feet-first slide. It enables the base runner to get to the base quicker, because he doesn't have to shift his weight back to get into the sitting position required in the feet-first slide. He simply has to lower his upper body and let gravity take over. He explodes—naturally and directly—into the base. It is also safer, because the base runner doesn't have to worry about catching the spikes.

Besides being simpler, safer and quicker, the headfirst slide seems to be more deceptive. Watch the umpires on a close call. If the tag is made on the elbow, the umpires tend to assume that the hand slid under the tag.

Of course, there are situations when the headfirst slide is inadvisable—for example, at home with the catcher blocking the plate. This slide now becomes dangerous. Another example is in breaking up a double play at second. The slider's head and hand become dangerously exposed to the pivot man's spikes.

Figure 8.8a

b

c

d

Figure 8.9a

b

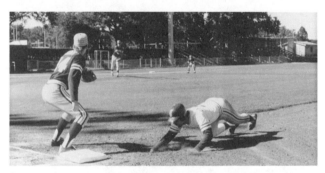

c

d

COACHING POINT

The headfirst slide, if taught properly, is more advantageous to the base-stealer than the feet-first slide. The bent-leg slide is also a valuable slide to learn, but after it is learned, the player must advance to the others.

Mental Aspects for Players

Instruct your players to keep the following ideas in mind about sliding:

- Don't be afraid to slide.
- When you make up your mind to slide, don't change it at the last second.
- Try not to slow down when you slide, but rather accelerate into the base.
- When you slide, try to concentrate on where the ball goes or ends up.

DRILLS

Bent-Leg Headfirst Drill

PURPOSE: To teach players the proper technique in sliding and to take the fear out of sliding. This drill
is especially valuable as a rainy-day drill.

EQUIPMENT: Throw-down bases, grassy area

IMPLEMENTATION:

1. Make sure you wet down the area without getting too
   much standing water.
2. Have players pair up and practice, one player sitting
   down, first on his side (Figure 8.10a) and then on his
   buttocks extending the lead leg and tucking the other
   under (Figure 8.10b), while the other pulls him several feet. Have players take turns pulling and sliding.
3. Players will immediately learn that it's easier to slide
   on their buttocks rather than on their side.
4. Have each player try each variation of the bent-leg
   slide.
5. Have each player try the headfirst slide.

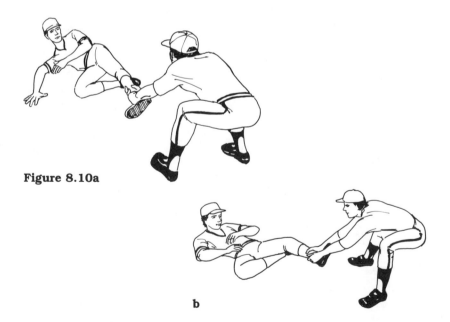

Figure 8.10a

b

Bent-Leg/Pop-Up, Headfirst, Back-Door, Pop-Tag Drill

PURPOSE: Reviews all the slides and steals.

EQUIPMENT: Infield and bases

IMPLEMENTATION:

1. Divide players into four groups. See Figure 8.11.
2. Put a group at home, first, second, and third.
3. Rotate groups after a 15-minute session.
4. Have the group at home work on reading the first baseman coming off the bag and avoiding a tag using the pop-tag method.
5. Have the group at first steal second, working on either a bent-leg or pop-tag.
6. Have the second baseman/shortstop simulate an overthrow and the runner use the pop-up slide.
7. Have the group at second steal third using the head-first slide.
8. Have the group at third work on stealing home using the pop-up.
9. Also have the group at third work on the pop-tag and back-door as if they were scoring from second.

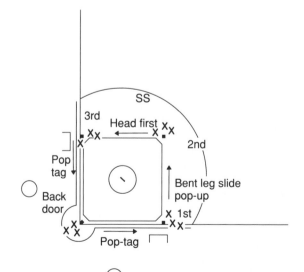

Figure 8.11

Diving Back Into First Base Drill

PURPOSE: To teach players the proper technique in diving back into first base.

EQUIPMENT: Throw-down bases, grassy area

IMPLEMENTATION:

1. Make sure to wet down an area lightly where the players are going to slide. This keeps them from getting abrasions while sliding.
2. Have players divide up into four separate stations.
3. Have your players use the right-field line as first base, take a lead, and then dive back on a coach's command.
4. It should require a step and a dive for the players to reach the base.
5. In a gym, the players can also slide in their socked feet and long pants.

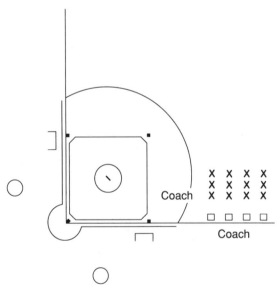

Figure 8.12

Index

A

Advancing from third to home, 125-142
  coaching points for, 126, 130, 131, 132, 136
  drills for, 141-142
  ground-ball situations, 129-130
  mental aspects for players, 139-140
  returning to the base, 129
  squeeze plays, 133-134
  stealing home, 134-139
  tagging up on fly balls, 131-133
  walking lead, 126-128
Advancing to Second Base Drill, 63
Aggressive running from first to second, 85-105
  coaching points for, 86, 90, 96, 97, 101
  delayed steal, 96-101
  drills for, 103-105
  fly balls, 101-102
  mental aspects for players, 102
  returning to first base, 94-96
  running against the clock, 86-87
  stealing second base, 87-94
Angle, for bunting, 35-36
Arm action, for stealing second base, 92-93

B

Base hit bunts from the left side, 42-45
  coaching point for, 43
Base hit bunts from the right side, 38-42
  coaching points for, 39, 40
Baserunning
  See also Advancing from third to home; Aggressive running from first to second; Getting to first base; Going from second to third
  against the clock, 86-87
  checking outfielders' arms, 59
  on fly balls, 101-102, 113-114, 131-133
  going for two, 59-60
  with a ground ball in the infield, 56-57
  with a ground ball through the infield, 57-59
  importance of, 53-54

prompt start essential to, 55-56
reading throws important to, 60
starting in the dugout, 54
studying the pitcher, 54
veering at first base, 57
winning games, 53-54, 60
Baserunning Drills, 121-123
Bat position, 8-9
Bat selection, 3-4
Batter's box, 9-10
Bent-Leg Headfirst Drill, 160
Bent-Leg/Pop-Up, Headfirst, Back-Door, Pop-Tag Drill, 161
Bent-leg slide, 144-146
  back-door slide with bent leg, 148, 150
  breaking up the double play via, 152-154
  coaching points for, 146, 150
  flip-flop slide with bent leg, 148, 150
  at home and at first, 150-152
  hook slide with bent leg, 147-148
  pop-up slide with bent leg, 146-147
Breaking balls, and batter's location in box, 9
Bunt and steal, 112-113
  coaching point for, 113
Bunting, 29-52
  base hit bunts from the left side, 42-45
  base hit bunts from the right side, 38-42
  bat in front of plate for, 36
  coaching point for, 30
  contribution of, to winning, 29
  deadening the ball, 37, 44-45
  down third-base line, 38-39
  drag bunt, 39-40, 42-43
  drills for, 49-52
  fake bunt, 45-46
  with first baseman playing deep, 40, 42
  knee position for, 37
  mental aspects for players, 48
  perfect or foul rule for, 38, 45
  pivot method, 33-34, 46, 47
  psychological barrier to, 30

About the Author

R od Delmonico is the head baseball coach at the University of Tennessee and one of college baseball's brightest young coaches. In his second year at Tennessee, Delmonico set a school record with a 41-19 record. He also spent 6 years as the head assistant coach with Florida State University, where he helped coach the team to three college world series.

Delmonico, who received his master's degree in education from Clemson University in 1983, is a member of the American Baseball Coaches Association. Delmonico has written extensively for *Scholastic Coach* since 1980 and, in a 10-year period, has published over 40 articles in numerous other magazines.